GUIDE

OF

ROME

THE ETERNAL CITY

Nine Itineraries

ROME
THE VATICAN
THE SISTINE CHAPEL

ALSO AVAILABLE IN:
ITALIAN - FRENCH - GERMAN - SPANISH
JAPANESE - POLISH - RUSSIAN

LOZZI *Roma*
edizioni turistiche

Direzione e redazione:
LOZZI ROMA s.a.s.
Via Filippo Nicolai, 91 - 00136 ROMA
Tel. (+39) 0635497051 - Fax (+39) 0635497074
www.lozziroma.com
e-mail: lozzirm@tiscaline.it

ROMA LA CITTÀ ETERNA
Periodico annuale.
Anno VI - Edizione 2002
Registrazione presso il Tribunale di Roma n° 625 del 13 XII 1996

Direttore responsabile *Franco Rossi Marcelli*

Stampato presso Arti grafiche F. Garroni
Via P. Santacroce, 47
00167 Roma

Fotolito Prima Print s.n.c.

Fotografie:
Archivio fotografico LOZZI ROMA s.a.s.
Archivio fotografico Millenium s.r.l.
Archivio fotografico Fabbrica di San Pietro
Archivio fotografico Musei e Gallerie Pontificie
La fotografia in copertina e quelle alle pag. 17 - 32 - 84
sono state gentilmente offerte dalla ROLO BANCA 1473

La Lozzi Roma s.a.s. è a disposizione degli aventi diritto per quanto
riguarda le fonti iconografiche non individuate.

GENERAL INDEX

ALPHABETICAL INDEX

BRIEF HISTORICAL OUTLINES

Rome is situated 41° 53' 54" N. lat., and 12° 59' 53" E. long., on the banks of the River Tiber.

According to Varro's calculations, Rome was founded on April 21, 753 B.C.

Rome was first governed by Kings (753-510 B.C.); then as a Republic by Consuls (510-30) and finally by Emperors (30 B.C. to 476 A.D.). During the Middle Ages, the Church established its temporal rule and Rome remained the seat of the Papal Court until September 20, 1870 when the Italian army entered Rome and the Eternal City became the capital of a united Italy.

The Vatican, a small territory of 0,440 Kms^2 occupied by St. Peter's Basilica, St. Peter's Square and the Vatican Palaces, is under the sovereignty of the Pope, and it has been called the "Vatican City State" since 1929.

Rome has a population of over three and a half million.

The Kings of Rome. According to the legend, the seven Kings of Rome were: Romulus, Numa Pompilius, Tullus Hostilius, Ancus Martius, Tarquinius Priscus, Servius Tullius, and Tarquinius the Proud.

667. Romans and Albans contesting for superiority agreed to choose three champions on each side to decide the question. The three Horatii, Roman knights, overcame the three Curiatii, Alban knights, and unite Alba to Rome.

509. Tarquin the Proud and his family expelled for tyranny and licentiousness; royalty abolished; the Patricians established an aristocratic commonwealth.

The Republic. First period (510-87 B.C.) from the expulsion of Tarquin to the Dictatorship of Sylla. - Second period (87-30 B.C.) from Sylla to Augustus.

496. The Latins and the Tarquins declared war against the Republic and were defeated at Lake Regillus.

477-396. Wars with Veii and the Etruscans. Veii taken by Camillus after ten years' siege.

390. The Gauls, under Brennus, won a remarkable victory over the Romans on the banks of the little River Allia, after which they sacked and plundered Rome. However, they eventually returned to their own land and Rome was gradually rebuilt.

343-290. The Samnitic Wars.

312-308. The Censor Appius Claudius built the first important main road, famous Appian Way and the first Roman aqueduct.

264-146. The Punic Wars, which culminated in the destruction of Carthage, the leading naval power in the Mediterranean.

146. The conquest of Greece.

88-86. Fighting between Marius and Sylla.

82-79. Sylla's dictatorship. Decline of the Republican institutions.

60-53. The First Triumvirate: Caesar, Pompey and Crassus.
58. Caesar's campaigns in Gaul and Britain.
48. Pompey was defeated at Pharsalus.
Caesar was assasinated on March15, 44 (the Ides of March), during a Senate Meeting.
43. The Second Triumvirate: Octavian (the future Augustus), Anthony and Lepidus.
42. Battle of Philippi in Macedonia. Death of Brutus and Cassius.
31. Octavian defeated Anthony and Cleopatra at Actium (Greece); remaining the sole ruler of Rome.

The Empire. The Emperor Octavian (63 B.C. - 14 A.D.) took the name of "Caesar Augustus". The birth of Jesus Christ.
The reign of Augustus coincided with the golden age of Latin literature: this was the era of writers such as Cicero, Virgil, Lucretius, Horace, Ovid, Livy and Tacitus.
61. St. Paul visited Rome for the first time, entering the city by the ancien Capena gate. During Nero's persecution (64-68) he was martyrized at same time as St. Peter.
64. Rome was burned in a great fire in Nero's reign and the Christians were blamed for the great fire.
70. Jerusalem was razed to the ground by Titus. Vespasian began to build the Colosseum in 72.
98-117. Under Trajan, the Roman Empire reached its maximum expansion.
117-138. during Hadrian's reign, Rome was at the peak of its architectural splendour.
The Empire began to decline between the 2nd and 3rd centuries, as a result of internal crises and because of pressure from barbarian peoples.
272. Aurelius began to build the Aurelian Walls as protection against the threat of invasion.
284. Diocletian and Maximian: the first division of the Empire.
312. Constantine the Great allowed the Christians freedom of religious practice. In 331 he transferred the capital of the Empire to Byzantium (Constantitople).
361. Julian the Apostate abjured Christianity and re-opened the pagan temples. He was killed in battle in Persia.
395. The Roman Empire was definitively divided between the East (Arcadius) and the West (Honorius).
404. Transfer of the Capital to Ravenna.
410. Rome sacked by the Goths.
475. Romulus Augustulus, the last Emperor.
476. Odoacer's conqueror of Rome put an end to the Roman Empire in the West.

The Middle Ages. 493. The Goths established their reign in Italy, defeating Odoacer.
535-553. the Byzantine-Gothic war.
568. The Lombards invaded Italy. It was divided among the Barbarians and the Eastern Empire (the Byzantines).

729. With the donation of Sutri by the Lombard king Liutprandus, the temporal rule of the popes began.

800. On Christmas day, Leo III crowned Charlemagne Emperor of the Holy Roman Empire.

1073-1085. Pope Gregory VII, a fervent and energetic reformer, began his fight against the Emperor Henry IV.

1084. Rome was invaded and sacked by the Romans, led by Robert the Guiscard.

1300. Boniface VIII proclaimed the first Jubilee.

1305. Clement V moved the papal seat from Rome to Avignon, where it remained until 1377.

The Renaissance. 1471. The foundation of the Capitoline Museum, the oldest public collection in the world.

1503-1513. Julius II began to pull down the old St. Peter's in order to build the present Basilica, under Bramante's supervision. The dawn of the Renaissance.

1513-1521. Leo X, the son of Lorenzo the Magnificent, made Rome the greatest cultural centre. - Under the pontificate of Leo X the Lutheran Reform began. - The imperial invasion of Italy and the disastrous Sack of Rome (16 May, 1527) put an end to the golden age of the papal city in a nightmare of fire and blood.

1585-1590. Sixtus V, a real innovator of town planning, covered Rome with new buildings.

The Modern and Contemporary Age. 1799. The Jacobine Republic in Rome, pope Pius VI was deported to France.

1800. The First Restoration: Pius VII was restablished in Rome.

1849. French troops put an end to the Republican government after seven months, and restored Pius IX to the papal throne.

1861. On March 27, the Italian Parliament declared Rome the natural and indispensable capital of the new State.

1870. On September 20, Italian troops entered Rome through the breach in Porta Pia.

1929. On February 11, the "Roman Question" between the Church and the State was finally resolved by the Lateran Treaty, which came to be part of the Constitution of the Italian Republic.

1943. The neighbourhood of St. Lawrence, was particularly damaged by bombing during the 2nd World War and there were many victims.

1946. In Italy, the Republic was proclaimed in accordance with the June 2 referendum.

1962-65. The Ecumenical Council, Vatican II, was summoned by John XXIII and concluded by Paul VI.

1978. After the death of Paul VI and the pontificate of John Paul I which lasted one month, John Paul II the Polish Pope, acceded to the pontifical throne. He is the first non-Italian Pope for more than four and a half centuries.

2000. Great celebration of the Holy Year.

1st itinerary
(see map)

Around the Capitol

The Capitoline Hill · The Imperial Forums
The Colosseum · The Roman Forum · The Palatine

The Capitol, once sacred to the Romans and the destination of the triumphal processions of victorious generals, is today the headquarters of the Mayor and the Municipality of Rome. In spite of changing events and historic conditions, the **CAPITOLINE HILL** has remained the basic nucleus of Roman life for thousands of years. It is reached by the grand flight of steps known as the "Cordonata", built to a design by Michelangelo especially for the triumphal entry of the Emperor Charles V in 1536.

The bronze statue of **Cola di Rienzo,** is by Masini. It is placed to the left of the Cordonata on fragments of ancient remains, to show that the last Roman Tribune wanted to re-establish the Republic on the ruins of the Empire. Cola was the son of an innkeeper. By reading the Latin classics as well as he could, he filled his mind with the glory and greatness of Rome: this glory he determined to restore. The statue was erected in 1887 presumably on the spot where the Tribune was killed by the people. At the top of the stairs are the colossal groups of the **Dioscuri**, Castor and Pollux, found near the Ghetto and placed here in 1583 by Gregory XIII. Sixtus V added the **Trophies of Marius** and the **statues of Constantine** and his son Constantine Caesar.

We now reach **Piazza del Campidoglio**, designed by Michelangelo for the munificent Pope Paul III (1534-1549). The old artist placed on a new pedestal the equestrian statue of **Marcus Aurelius** (161-180), the only one of the many bronze equestrian statues once adorning Rome that has survived.

Because the statue was thought for centuries to have represented the first Christian Emperor, Constantine, it escaped the fate of many other statues of pagan emperors, which were destroyed in the Middle Ages.

The completely gilded statue stood at the Lateran in the House of Vero, ancestor of Marcus Aurelius, until Michelangelo had it removed in 1538. In 1997 a copy took the place of the original, which after a lengthy and delicate restoration was moved to a protected display in the courtyard of the adjacent Capitoline Museum.

This splendid square was conceived by Michelangelo, who also designed the two palaces on the opposite sides of the square, whose divergence creates a widening perspective which is most effective.

The **Palazzo Senatorio** at the back of the square, was built in the 13th century on the ancient ruins of the Tabularium. Its present façade was designed by Giacomo della Porta and made by Girolamo Rainaldi. Michelangelo designed the flight of steps. The fountain, adorned with three statues, the **Tiber** and the **Nile** on either side and **Rome Triumphant** (of over modest proportions) in the centre, was added in 1588 by Matteo di Castello. The Senator's Palace is the Mayor's resi- dence. Rising from it is the **Capitoline Tower**, built in 1579 by Martino Longhi, where the famous bell, the "Patarina", once hung.

The two lateral palaces house the **CAPITOLINE MUSEUM** which contains a very rich collection of classical marbles, the oldest public collection in the world (1471).

In the courtyard of the **Palazzo Nuovo**, on the left for those who have climbed the "Cordonata", we see among other things, the statue of Marforio, one of the "talking" statues of Rome, like the more famous Pasquino. A broad stairway leads to the first floor.

In the centre of the first room, the **Dying Gaul** lies in agony, a marble copy of the bronze statue of the Hellenistic King Attalus I of Pergamon (3rd century B.C.); the simple, natural position of the body, the features of the face which express deep anguish while they reveal human strength, everything blends marvellously to make this statue one of the most sig- nificant examples of Hellenistic sculpture.

The well known group of **Love and Psyche**, an enchanting Hellenistic work, shows the chaste kiss of young lovers. The sculpture is a copy of a 2nd century original.

The Satyr is the best copy of an original bronze statue by Praxiteles, who had the divine gifts of tender beauty and grace.

Second and third rooms: various sculptured works of art. The fourth, or philosophers' room, contains many busts of Greek and Roman writers and warriors. In the centre, the seated statue is believed to be **M. Claudius Marcellus**, one of the Roman generals of the Second Punic War who, after a long siege, occupied Syracuse, where the famous great scientist Archimedes rendered useless the powerful machine of the Romans. Among the many busts, four are of the great epic poet of Greece, **Homer**, who sang the heroes of Troy, and was disputed as citizen by seven cities. Tradition represents him as a poor blind man. **Socrates**, the celebrated Athenian philosopher, is here with his flat nose, thick lips, protruding eyes, like a satyr. Before drinking the fatal poisoned cup, he had already set forth his idea of the immortality of the soul.

The fifth room, or room of the Emperors, contains about eighty busts of Roman Emperors and Empresses; it is the most interesting portrait gallery in existence. The name of Caesar is commonly given to the first twelve Emperors. These who, when we were in school, seemed like myths to us now become men of yesterday through their life-like busts in this room. Art has made them our contemporaries.

"The Room of Venus". The **Capitoline Venus** was found at Suburra in the 17ᵗʰ century. It is perhaps the most pleasing preservation of all the goddesses; here we admire her in all her beauty, full of charm and grace. It is in the style of Praxiteles.

"The Room of the Doves". The **mosaic of the Doves** was found in Hadrian's Villa at Tivoli and was at once recognized as the one described by the naturalist Plinius. It might even be taken for a painting, so fine is the work.

In the lovely figure of a **Maiden clasping a dove to her breast** when attacked by a snake, we see a symbol of the human soul in the choice between good and evil.

The Palace of the Conservatori contains innumerable artistic treasures.

The first room was painted by Giuseppe Cesari, Cav. d'Arpino. He worked here for more than forty years. The other rooms were painted by Laurenti, Daniele da Volterra, Caracci, etc.

The admirable statue of the **Cavaspina** (Boy extracting a thorn from his foot) in the third room, belongs to the pre-Phidian period. It is probably the best surviving statue of that time.

The **She-wolf** (fourth room), the symbol of Rome, is an Etruscan work which dates from the 5th century B.C. In the 15th century, during the first flowering of the Renaissance, the Tuscan scupltor, Pollaiolo added the figures of two babies, who represent Romulus and Remus.

Bust of Homer.

Young girl with dove.

Love and Psyche.

Dying Gaul.

Capitoline Venus.

Removing a thorn.

St. John The Baptist by Caravaggio.

The PINACOTECA CAPITOLINA picture gallery, contains some important masterpieces, among others: Romulus and Remus, by Rubens; Cleopatra and Antonius, by Guercino; The Rape of Europe, by Paolo Veronese; St. Sebastian, by Guido Reni; St. Petronilla, by Guercino; Magdalene, by Tintoretto; portraits by Van Dyck, etc.

SANTA MARIA IN ARACOELI rises on the highest point of the Capitol, site of the Rock or Citadel of Rome. A legend relates that Augustus raised an altar here to the "Son of God", to recall the oracle of the Sibyl about the coming of the Saviour. This church inherited the glory of the ancient Capitol; it became the national church of the nobility and people of Rome, the principal seat of the medieval Senate, whence the laws of Rome were proclaimed.

The "Capitoline Basilica" is very picturesque with its secular relics, its tombs, its frescoes, its gilded ceiling and ancient trappings. It originally belonged to the Greek monks, then to the Benedictine Fathers until 1250, when it was given to the Franciscans. It is reached by a staircase of 124 steps that was built in 1348 as an offering to the Blessed Virgin for freeing Rome from the plague.

High up is the (incomplete) brick **facade**, with traces of late 2nd century mosaics on the upper right.

We enter by a side door, above which is the most lovely 13th century mosaic depicting the **Madonna and Child** and two angels. The nave has twenty-two columns made from different materials, taken from various pagan temples. The third column on the left bears the inscription "A cubicolo Augustorum".

The elaborate sixth-century gold-coffered **ceiling** was built to celebrate the triumph of Marcantonio Colonna, who in 1571 led the Christian fleet to victory over the Turks in the famous Battle of Lepanto.

The first chapel on the right of the nave is dedicated to **St. Bernadino of Siena** and was decorated by Pinturicchio for Nicola Bufalini of Città di Castello, in memory of the peace achieved by St. Bernadino between the two powerful rival families, the Baglioni and the Bufalini. These frescoes are thought to date from 1497 to 1500. St. Bernadino can be seen opposite, between St. Anthony of Padua and St. Ludovico of Toloso, crowned with angels. The fresco on the left portrays the funeral of the saint: it shows some very beautiful heads, many of which are portraits of the Bufalini. The four noble figures of the Evangelists are painted on the vault. In the "Chapel of St. Francis" on the right of the transept, are the tombs of the Savelli. The **monument to Luca Savelli** (13th century) is a richly decorated Roman sarcophagus upon which was laid another, decorated in mosaics, with three Savelli coats of arms.

The Aracoeli Madonna on the main altar, an interesting picture in the Byzantine style, is attributed to St. Luke. In fact, it is a painting on wood which scholars have dated variously, from the 6th to the 11th centuries.

In the choir, on the left is the **tomb of Cardinal Giovanni Battista Savelli**, the work of Andrea Bregno's school (15th century).

The **richly decorated Ambos** at the back of the central nave, are the work of Lorenzo Cosmati and his son Jacopo, whose signature is visible on the righthand side of the pulpit.

On the left of the transept, the octagonal chapel dedicated to **St. Helena** marks the place of the other altar of the Augustan legend. Right under the altar of St. Helena, at a level 15 cm. (6 in.) lower than the present pavement, there is a white marble altar, embellished with sculptures and mosaics. They illustrate scenes of the above mentioned legend which can be interpreted with the help of the scenes on the table of the altar. It dates from the 12th century. The slim statue of the Saint is a contemporary work by Andrea Martini (1972).

Close by is the **tomb of Matteo Acquasparta**. General of the Franciscans in 1287, he was reprimanded by Dante in his "Divine Comedy", for being responsible for relaxing the Rule. It is an interesting monument in the Gothic style, adorned with a fresco by the greatest Roman painter of the 13th century, Pietro Cavallini; it shows the **Madonna and Child** flanked by two saints.

PIAZZA VENEZIA, the heart of Rome and the heart of Italy, takes its name from the **Palazzo Venezia** which the Venetian Paul II (1461-1471), a lover of munificence, had built in 1455 while he was still a cardinal. It was the first great Renaissance palace of Rome, and its was enriched by outstanding art works. It was a typical example of this first Renaissance period and it marked the transition to a modern palace from the mediaeval fortified dwelling place, of which it retains certain features.

The **Victor Emmanuel II Monument *** also called the "Vittoriano", was designed by Giuseppe Sacconi (1885-1911).

It rises at the foot of the Capitol in the heart of Rome, where it was squeezed in, altering the ancient relationship between this hill and the neighbouring district, with its massive dimensions. The Venetian sculptor Chiaradia, worked for twenty years on the equestrian statue of the King which was completed after his death by Gallori (1901). The elaborate bas-reliefs at the base which represent the most illustrious Italian cities, were designed by Maccagnani, who for many years collaborated with Sacconi in carving the three-dimensional ornaments. The building's two colossal **wings** are surmounted by winged victories, whose dark bronze contrasting with the bright marble and clearly visible against the panorama of Rome, were made in 1908 by Carlo Fontana and Paolo Bartolini. In the centre is the **Altar of the Fatherland** crowned by the statue of Rome at whose feet since 1921, lies the **Tomb of the Unknown Soldier.**

To the left of the "Vittoriano" is a **fragment of a tomb** in travertine marble, which was erected to Caius Publicius Bibulos "for his honour and courage" as the inscription states (1st century B.C.). From the square begins the **Via dei Fori Imperiali,** a broad, straight stretch built in 1932, cutting through the ruins of the forums from which it takes its name. A proposal has recently been made to completely close this artery to traffic and to continue with the excavations, a fascinating project and a tough challenge which would make this zone one of the most precious archeological sites in the world.

Julius Caesar's Forum was the first of the so-called "Imperial Forums", built using the spoils from the victories of the Gallic wars. On August 9, 48 B.C., the decisive battle was fought at Pharsalus between Caesar's formidable army, triumphantly returning from Gaul, and that of his rival Pompey, who was contesting his primacy in what was already by then the dying Roman Republic. Victorious once again, Caesar built a new forum between the old Republican Forum (which had become too small), and the Quirinal, with the **Temple to Venus Genetrix** in the centre. The Julia family to which Caesar belonged, in fact boasted their descent from Julius or Ascanius, the son of the Trojan hero Aeneas, who, according to Homeric mythology, was born to the mortal Anchises and the goddess Venus. Many Venus Gentrix sculpted by Arcileus who was one of the most

Aerial view of the Capitol.

celebrated Greek sculptors, and a portrait of Cleopatra. The Temple was rebuilt by Trajan and inaugurated, together with Trajan's column, on May 12, 113.

TRAJAN'S FORUM. The Emperor M. Ulpius Trajan was born in Italica (Spain) in 53 B.C. The formidable task accomplished in his reign was the conquest of Dacia (present day Romania). In 101 he began his campaign: when the roads and fortifications were ready, Trajan took the capital by force and imposed impossibly hard conditions which Decebalus, the leader of the Dacians, did not choose to abide by. In 105 fighting was resumed. The Dacians fought desperately: "to victory or to death"; but their army was wiped out. Their heroic prince commited suicide and Trajan returned to Rome laden with treasures. After the celebrations of his triumph, he wished to remember his victory and decided to build a forum which would surpass all others in size and splendour. He entrusted this task to the great architect Apollodorus of Damascus. The new forum became the most admired place in the city. There were two libraries, a commemorative column, a basilica, a temple, a great equestrian statue of Trajan and a triumphal arch: there was a profusion of statues and groups. Towards the middle of the 4th century, the Emperor Constantius of the East visited Rome, accompanied by the Persian Prince Orsmida. When they reached Trajan's Forum, he was so astonished at the sight of the incredible creation that he exclaimed: "It would be impossible for me even to try to imitate it; at most I would be able to make the horse!" And the Prince observed: "Your Majesty, for such a horse, you would first need a stable like that!".

But the great Monument of the Dacian War is the noble **Column** that still rises in its pristine majesty, bathed in the glory of more than nineteen centuries.

The ashes of the Emperor were placed at the foot of the monument and his statue on top of it. The column consists of 19 blocks of marble and a spiral staircase leads to the top. The most important part of this historic monument is the helicoidal band of figures going all around it which gives us a documentary view of the arms, arts and costumes of both the Romans and the Dacians. Here we see the bridges Trajan built, the forts he attacked, the camps he destroyed, the enemy he put to flight. The old interpretations of the inscriptions on the column have now been recognized as exact. The column shows how deep an exca-

vation was dug to make place for the Ulpia Basilica.
Very little remains of the great buildings which surrounded the Column, the **Basilica Ulpia**, destined for the administration of justice, the two **libraries** Greek and Latin and the **temple** dedicated to Trajan himself. Besides the wear and tear of the years, the wide stretch of the adjacent Via dei Fori Imperiali which was made in 1932-1933, conceals a large part of this Forum from our sight.
The complex of **Trajan's markets** was erected on the face of the Quirinal hill which was cut through to build the Forum. The two groups of which it consists, a lower construction framed by a semi-circle on three floors, extremely well preserved, and an upper one which contains a large vaulted hall as well as other rooms, which resembles a basilica. These buildings form a marvellous group in which their archeological merits blend with the landscape, making them a real pleasure to the eye. The well preserved state of this complex makes it ideal for exhibitions and cultural events. The entrance is at the side, through a gate opening on to Via IV Novembre, which can be reached up the steps from Via Magnanapoli.

The Forum of Augustus. After Caesar's assassination, Brutus and Cassius, the main culprits, went to the East to take possession of the provinces of Syria and Macedonia. In 42 B.C. they led their armies into battle at Philippi, against the heirs of Caesar, Octavian and Marcus Aurelius. And just as Julius Caesar had taken a vow at Pharsalus, so Augustus took one at Philippi: in the event of victory, he was to dedicate a temple to Mars, the father of the Roman people, in a new forum. After the victory and the death of the two conspirators, built the **Temple of Mars Ultor** (the Conqueror), in the centre of the new Forum, dedicated to him and inaugurated on the first day of the month of August in the year 2 B.C. The excavations have brought to light magnificent remains of this Forum and the gigantic temple, which Ovid described.

The Forum of Nerva. Began by the Emperor Domitian, this Forum was inaugurated in 97 A.D. by his successor Nerva after whom it is called. Built after the Forums of Caesar and Augustus, it was necessary to make the best of a rather limited space, and so it extended in length rather than in breadth. This was the site of the **Temple of Minerva**, which was still standing until 1606 when Pope Paul V had it

The Basilica of Santa Maria in Aracoeli

The Basilica of Santa Maria in Aracoeli - Inside.

demolished in order to use its marble for building the Pauline fountain on the Janiculum.

The Temple of Peace. The complex of the Imperial Forums ended towards the Colosseum, with this temple of enormous proportions. Several remains have been found close to the current side-entrance of the Roman Forum, in the gardens in front of the Basilica of Maxentius, and in the Church of St. Cosmos and St. Damian.

At the end of the Via dei Fori Imperiali stands the **COLOSSEUM** *, one of the greatest marvels of the Roman civilization.
This immense amphitheatre, whose ancient splendour we can still admire was begun by Vespasian in A.D. 72 and finished by his son Titus in A.D. 80. Hebrew prisoners were employed in its construction. Its real name is the **Flavian Amphitheatre**, commonly called Coloseum perhaps because the Colossus of Nero was in its vicinity. There is scarcely a page of Roman history that is not connected with the Colosseum, which became the symbol of the city and its life. Thus in the 8th century the Venerable Bede said: "While the Colosseum stands, Rome shall stand; when the Colosseum falls, Rome shall fall; and when Rome falls, with it the World shall fall". After the sacking of the Normans (1084), nothing but a skeleton remained of antique classic Rome; the Colosseum was abandoned and for years it was used as a quarry for building material.
To save what was left of it, Benedict XIV (1740-1758) consecrated the ancient amphitheatre by setting up a permanent **Way of the Cross** and erecting a cross on this site, which the pius legend has linked with the name of the thousands of martyrs who gave up their lives for their faith. In fact, there is no historical proof that Christian massacres took place here even though many Christians were certainly among those who were put to death in this monument.
The "Ludi Circernses" were the favourite shows of the Romans, games that were probably invented in the last days of the Republic, with the intention of developing the warlike spirit that had made them the conquerors of the world. This was the origin of the professional gladiators, who were trained to fight to the death, while wild beasts of every sort increased the horror of the show. Dion Cassius says that 9000 wild animals were killed during the hundred days of festivity to celerate the dedication of this building. After

← *Piazza Venezia and Via dei Fori Imperiali - Aerial view.*

the animals were killed, and removed, the arena was often filled with water in order to stage naval battles. The great Emperor Constantine and his successors tried to stop the gladiatorial fights, but at first the Romans would not give up their customary shows.

The last of these events about which we have some evidence, dates back to 523, when Theodoric, King of the Goths, agreed to an animal hunt requested by the consul elected for that year.

The Colosseum, of elliptical form, is 205 yards in its longest diameter and 170 yards in its shortest. On the outside there were three rows of arches, respectively adorned with Doric, Ionic and Corinthian columns, and a fourth floor was adorned with Corinthian pilasters. An ellipse of 80 arches formed the outer circuit. Four arches corresponding to the four semi-diameters led to a large corridor that went all around it. In the centre of one side of the podium called "suggestum", was the Emperor's seat; the rest of the podium was occupied by senators and patricians. Then there were the places for cavaliers, civil and military tribunes. There were also special places for married people, for young men accompanied by their tutors, for families and servants, for women and for the plebeians.

The Colosseum was normally uncovered; but in the case of rain or during very hot days it was protected by an immense velarium, which was fixed by two squads of sailors belonging to the fleets of Ravenna and Capo Miseno.

These two teams also took part in naval battles, which were however soon moved to suitable pools close to the Tiber. Among them, the "Naumachia Vaticana" is famous. It was designed by Domitian himself, who was responsible for completing the Colosseum.

When the amphitheatre was at the climax of its glory, it must have been a stupendous sight of Roman splendour. But even to-day, after so many centuries, the Colosseum is the pride of Rome and the marvel of visitors.

Between the Colosseum, the Arch of Constantine and the south entrance to the Roman Forum, interesting excavations have been carried out, which have not only made it possible to replace well known monuments in their original locations, (at least ideally), such as the fountain of the **Meta Sudans** and the base of the **Colossos of Nero**, but have supplied numerous clues as to the way this area, including the complex of the **Domus Aurea** (Nero's Golden House),

The Monument to Victor Emmanuel II

The Trajan's Markets.

The Roman Forum with the Church of Santa Francesca Romana.

was organized. Before the rule of Nero, a district of rather small, irregular dwellings existed here, whose remains show the clearest traces of the fire of 64 A.D. After this dramatic event, Nero had an artificial lake made in this little valley, in the spot which was later occupied by the Colosseum.

The Arch of Constantine was erected by the Senate and the Roman people at the extreme limit of the Forum on the Via Sacra, in memory of Constantine's victory at Ponte Milvio in 312.

Almost all the material was taken from the arches of Trajan and Marcus Aurelius and from other monuments, so that this work may be considered "a true museum of official Roman sculpture, perhaps the richest and the most important of all" (F. Coarelli). From the historical point of view, the most interesting part of the arch is its inscription: «To the Emperor Caesar Flavius Constantine Maximus, "pius, felix, augustus", the Senate and the people of Rome dedicate this notable arch in honour of his triumphs, because, inspired by Divinity and greatness of mind, he freed the Republic by just wars from tyranny and from factions».

Now the magistrates of the city were pagans and they knew that Constantine, if not a Christian, favoured Christianity. They did not want to name Christ on a public monument and yet they did not want to offend the Emperor by naming pagan gods. So they found a way to satisfy both sides by saying "Divine inspiration".

In the adjoining convent, is the "Antiquarium Forense", in which objects of great interest from the excavations carried out in the Forum area are exhibited.

The finest religious building in Rome was the twin **Temple of Venus and Roma** of which the ruins still remain. The columns, scattered on the ground, and now reconstructed and erected on the same spot, give us the idea of the portico that surrounded the temple. It was designed by Hadrian, who had the "Colossus of Nero" removed to obtain the necessary space.

On the ruins of the Temple of Venus and Roma, was built, in the VII century, the church of "Santa Maria Nova", dedicated at the begining of the XVIII century to **Santa Francesca Romana**.

The Church and the Antiquarium are within the precinct of the **ROMAN FORUM ***, the monumental complex whose remains lie between the Capitol, the Imperial Forums, the Coosseum and the Palatine.

The Forum was crossed by the **Via Sacra** which led to the Capitoline hill and was the route of the triumphal processions of victorious generals, laden with booty and followed by their ranks of prisoners. While the most ancient section of the Forum, in the Republican epoch, stretched from the opposite side of the valley to the slopes of the Capitol, the entrance on the square of the Colosseum leads to the most recently built section, which dates from the Imperial age.

Another important street, the **Via Nova**, crossed the length of the valley along the slopes of the Palatine. In this area, until recently little explored, extremely interesting excavations are presently underway which show how, in the very heart of archeological Rome, it is still possible to make unexpected discoveries capable of shedding new light on our knowledge. The zone was largely built up after the death of Nero who had integrated this area into the grounds of his Golden House, at the request of the Emperor Vespasian, who made it, as we would say today, a real focal point of the city. On the adjacent northern slopes of the Palatine, exacavations have revealed a series of private dwellings from the Republican age, including the house of Cicero, who left us precise literary evidence describing this area as "pulcherrimus" (very beautiful).

On the Via Sacra, on the very top of the Velia, the **Arch of Titus**, erected by the Senate after the Emperor's death in memory of the conquest of Jerusalem (70 A.D), stands elegantly to welcome the visitor.

In the interior are two fine bas-reliefs: the Emperor on his triumphal chariot and the procession of Jewish prisoners carrying the famous candelabrum with seven branches.

The immense **Basilica of Maxentius**, also called Constantine's Basilica is the last edifice bearing the impression of the magnificence of ancient Rome. It was begun by Maxentius and finished after the victory by Constantine.

This magnificent 4th century construction, which is thought to have inspired Bramante in his design for the new St. Peter's, has been restored, revealing the part facing the Forum.

This is the lesser northern aisle, with its great apse and powerful vaulted domes which were a source of ispiration to the most admired Renaissance architects.

The **Temple of Antoninus and Faustina** (2nd century A.D.)

THE COLOSSEUM - PAST

THE COLOSSEUM - PRESENT

is best preserved in the Forum. The loss of Faustina embittered the Emperor, who often used to say he would have preferred to live in a desert with her than in a palace without her. After her death, the Emperor deified her and erected this magnificent temple in her honour.

Pagan temples were frequently converted into Christian churches. Even the ancient **Church of St. Cosma and St. Damian**, was built by Felix IV in 572, inside the "Templum Sacrae Urbis", which the Emperor Vespasian built in the adjacent "Forum of Peace", or "Vespasian's Forum", mainly hidden under the asphalt of the Via dei Fori Imperiali. The vestibule stands on the **"Tempietto Rotondo"** (Circular Temple) of Romulus, the son of Maxentius (4th century), and still preserves the bronze door with its original lock. The "Sepolcretum" or "Archaic Necropolis" dates to the 9th century B.C. Thus we have penetrated one of the oldest areas of the Forum. In fact, according to legend, the first foundations of the **Temple of Vesta** date from the time of King Numa Pompilio, (8th century B.C.). This is a circular building, whose purpose was to guard the Palladium (the image of Minerva) and other sacred objects brought to Italy, according to the legend, by Aeneas and upon which it was believed the security of the city depended.

The Vestals had to keep the fire burning. They were six, chosen from patrician maidens, daughters of free parents. They enjoyed special privileges, but if one broke the vow of chastity, she was buried alive in the Field of Villains. They lived close by in the **House of the Vestal Virgins**, which was almost totally reconstructed by the Emperor Septimius Severus after a fire in 191 A.D., as was the temple to the Goddess. Many statues and inscriptions can still be seen; on one of these, the name of a Vestal Virgin was cancelled, leaving only her initial, 'C'... It is quite likely that it was the Vestal Virgin Claudia, to whom a statue was erected in 364 as "homage to her chastity and deep knowledge of religion". Perhaps her name was cancelled because she converted to Christianity.

The **Temple of Julius Caesar** that Octavianus erected in memory of his uncle, was begun in B.C. 42 on the spot where the Dictator's body was burned, and consecrated in B.C. 29 at the same time as the Arch of Augustus of which only the foundations remain.

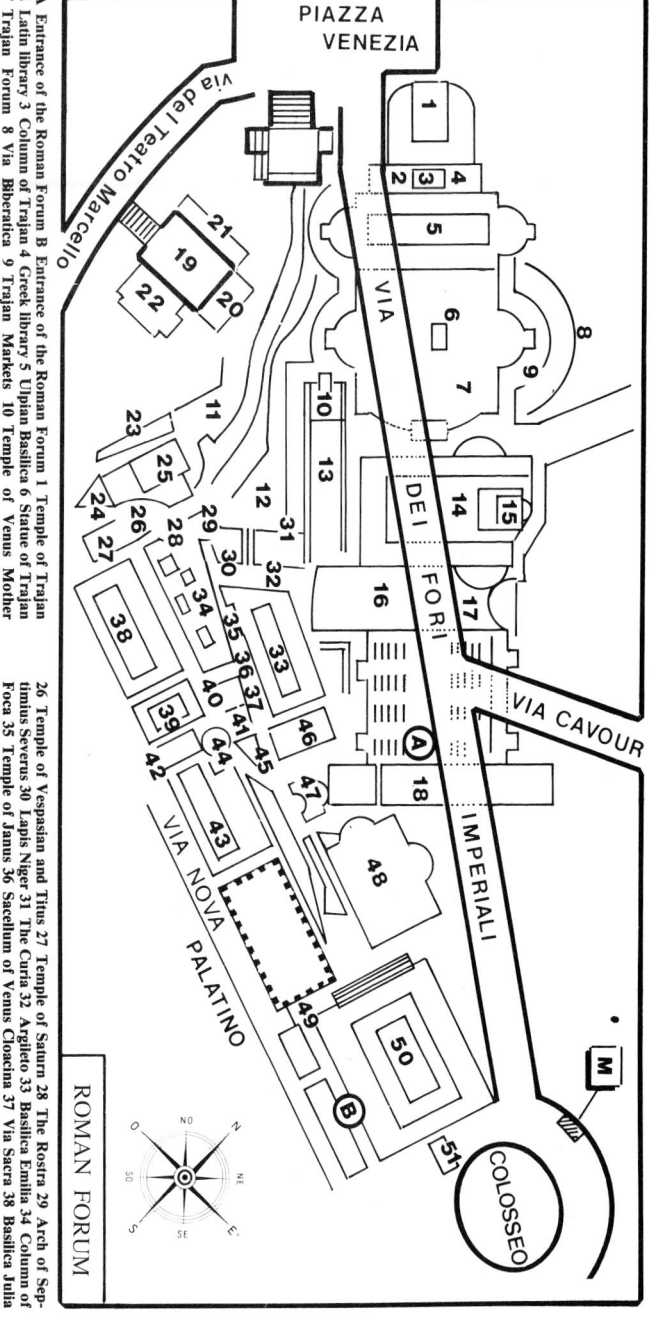

ROMAN FORUM

PIAZZA VENEZIA

Via del Teatro Marcello

VIA DEI FORI IMPERIALI

VIA CAVOUR

VIA NOVA

PALATINO

COLOSSEO

A Entrance of the Roman Forum B Entrance of the Roman Forum 1 Temple of Trajan 2 Latin library 3 Column of Trajan 4 Greek library 5 Ulpian Basilica 6 Statue of Trajan 7 Trajan Forum 8 Via Biberatica 9 Trajan Markets 10 Temple of Venus Mother 11 Mamertino Prison 12 The Comitium 13 Forum of Julius Caesar 14 Forum of Augustus 15 Temple of Mars Ultores 16 Forum of Nerva 17 Temple of Minerva 18 Temple of Peace 19 Capitol 20 Palace of the Senators 21 Capitoline Museum 22 Palace of the "Conservatori" 23 Tabularium 24 Portico of the Dii Consentes 25 Temple of Concordia

26 Temple of Vespasian and Titus 27 Temple of Saturn 28 The Rostra 29 Arch of Septimius Severus 30 Lapis Niger 31 The Curia 32 Argileto 33 Basilica Emilia 34 Column of Foca 35 Temple of Janus 36 Sacellum of Venus Cloacina 37 Via Sacra 38 Basilica Julia 39 Temple of Dioscuri 40 Arch of Augustus 41 Temple of Julius Caesar 42 Fountain of Juturna 43 House of the Vestal Virgins 44 Temple of Vesta 45 Royal Palace 46 Temple of Antoninus and Faustina 47 Temple of Romulus 48 Basilica of Maxentius 49 Arch of Titus 50 Temple of Venus and Roma 51 Arch of Constantine

The **Regia**, according to tradition, was the house of Numa Pompilius and, later, the residence of the "Pontifex Maximus". On the walls are the "fasti consolari" in sculpture.

The **Temple of Castor and Pollux**, also called the Temple of the Twins, was erected in B.C. 484 to celebrate the victory of Aulus Postumius over the Latins, in the battle at Lake Regillus. The three columns and part of the cornice, very fine work in Pentelic marble, are of the time of Trajan or Hadrian (1st or 2nd century A.D.).

St. Maria Antiqua is one of the oldest Roman basilicas built by transforming an imperial edifice annexed to the Atrium Minervae in the 5th century. The church consists of an atrium, a narthex, three naves and a presbytery. On the walls of the apse, we note the frescoes of the 8th century, greatly deteriorated. The church was buried by a landslide in the 9th century and was only brought to light by the excavations of 1900. —

The **Basilica Julia**, built according to the wishes of Julius Caesar in the middle of the 1st century B.C., was a grandiose building with five naves, divided into sectors with movable divisions which made it possible for more than one audience to take place at the same time. On the steps, and still visible today, there are vestiges of chess squares traced on the marble, a pleasurable passtime for the leisurely.

In 362 B.C. an abyss, called **Lacus Curtius**, opened in the centre of the Forum, which, according to the oracle, would not close again unless they would throw in it what Rome held most precious. Mettus Curius, deciding that nothing was more precious than a good citizen, mounting his horse in full armour, threw himself into the abyss which closed up forever. Many centuries afterwards, in this same spot, according to the Christian legend, the holy Pope Sylvester overcame the dragon whose pestilential breath killed the citizens. The Pope, cross in hand, threw a rope round the neck of the monster and dragged it into the abyss, which shut, never to open again paganism was overcome by the Cross.

The **Comitium**, the place where the representatives of the people gathered for public discussions, was also at first the tribunal of Rome. It was here, in the first days of the Republic, that Junius Brutus condemned to death his two sons, who had been denounced for plotting the return of King Tarquinius. Here the beautiful Virginia was stabbed

Aerial view of the Colosseum.

by her father. In this square, the most powerful voices of Rome resounded; Cicero, prince of orators, made his famous speeches of the second and third Catilinaria. Here the head of the great writer and politician was exposed to public view after his assassination.

The **Column of Phocas** is the last classical monument in the Forum. At the beginning of the 7th century, Phocas, the Emperor of Byzantium, allowed Pope Boniface IV to change the Pantheon into a Christian church. As a sign of gratitude, the Romans took a beautiful carved column from the portico of some ancient building and set it up here, putting the statue of the Byzantine sovereign on top.

The Arch of Septimius Severus, ornate to the point of being over-decorated, was erected in honour of Septimius and his two sons, Caracalla and Geta. The inscription recalls an imperial tragedy: after killing Geta, Caracalla had his brother's name removed.

Septimius Severus reigned 18 years (193-211) and died a natural death, a rare thing in the 3rd century. He had brilliant military successes everywhere. He was born at Leptis Magna in Africa and died in York (Eboracum), England.

The **Temple of Saturn** was erected by the Consul Titus Larcius on the 17th of December 498 B.C. It was always used as the Public Treasury. The ensigns of the Legions and decrees of the Senate were also kept here. In an underground cell were kept the sacred treasures, among which was the gold for ransom given to Brennus and reclaimed by the valour of Camillus.

In 42 B.C. the Temple was rebuilt on a larger scale. We see it today as it was reconstructed in the 4th century by the Christians for use as a Public Treasury.

The **Temple of Vespasian** was erected by his son, Domitian, in 94 and restored by Septimius Severus. Only three columns remain.

The **Temple of Concord** was built by Furio Camillo the conqueror of the Gauls in 367 B.C., in memory of the agreement made at Monte Sacro by the plebians and the patricians. This was the period when the Senate met to hear the last ''catilinaria'' of Cicero (63 B.C.).

The **Curia**, founded according to the legend by King Tullius Hostilius, (7th century B.C.) was the seat of the Roman Senate. Successively destroyed and rebuilt, and transformed in the Middle ages into a Christian church dedicated to St.

FORUM ROMANUM

1. *Curia*
2. *Arch of Septimius Severus*
3. *The Rostra*
4. *Arch of Tiberius*
5. *Via Sacra*
6. *Temple of Saturnus*
7. *Column of Phocas*
8. *Basilica Julia*
9. *Basilica Aemilia*
10. *Temple of Julius Caesar*
11. *Temple of Vesta*
12. *Temple of Castor and Pollux*
13. *St. Maria Antiqua*
14. *Temple of Augustus*
15. *Temple of Antoninus and Faustina*
16. *Temple of Romulus*
17. *Temple of Venus and Roma*
18. *House of the Virgin Vestals*
19. *Basilica of Maxentius*
20. *Colosseum*
21. *Arch of Titus*
22. *Palatinum*

Hadrian, in the 1930s it was restored to its original condition by a process which some experts consider to have been over drastic.

The **Basilica Emilia** was founded in 179 B.C. by Emilius Lepidus and Fulvius Nobilior. Rebuilt and restored several times, especially by the Aemilia family, it was definitively destroyed by fire in the beginning of the 5th century.

It was one of the most splendid buildings of the Forum, destined like all buildings of this type to serve as a centre for the legal and administrative procedures of the city.

In front of the Basilica is the small round pedestal of the shrine of Venus Cloacina on the spot where the Cloaca Maxima entered the Forum.

In the area behind the Curia and the Basilica Emilia, excavations by the municipal archeological authority of Rome in collaboration with the section of ancient topography of Rome's "La Sapienza" University, have led to the discovery of impressive foundations belonging to Nerva's Forum, as well as numerous preceding structures from the Republican era. One of the furnaces was also found in which, throughout the Middle Ages, the precious marbles were charred to reduce them to anonymous building material. The boundaries of the Forum valley are defined by the slopes of the Capitol at whose base interesting excavations are in progress, after the elimination of a through street in 1981. Stratigraphic excavation, carried out using the most modern methods, has made it possible to reconstruct the history of this area over the centuries, thereby establishing a useful testing ground for traditional Roman archeological historiography.

Another historic Roman hill, the **PALATINE**, looks over the Forum, preserving unforgettable memories in the greenery of its luxuriant vegetation.

During the Republic, the Patrician families dwelt on the Palatine. Quintus Hortensius, the celebrated orator who emulated Cicero, lived here in a house given him by Augustus. When Augustus became Emperor, he made his imperial residence on the Palatine. Afterwards Tiberius, Caligola, the Flavii and Septimius Severus built palaces here.

The Palatine was the cradle of Rome. Here, according to legend, Romulus traced the square out-line of the first city with a plough; here was the seat of the Kings. Because of this, the hill was chosen as the residence of the Caesars and Septimius Severus, no Emperor left it. Only Nero until built his Domus Aurea elsewhere but it was never finished nor inhabited by him.

On entering by the Arch of Titus, turning to the left, we climb on the right the **Clivus Palatinus** and following the stairs on the right, we reach the splendid Villa Farnese with its 16th century pavillion and gardens, supported by the powerful arches of the **Domus Tiberiana**. From the terrace on the left, we descend the steps to the Area Palatina, where among other venerable memories there are the ruins of the temple of the **Magna Mater** with the seated statue of Cibele, fragments of the walls of square Rome, some blocks of tufa supposed to belong to the hut of Romulus and traces of the **Scalae Caci**, the primitive access to the Palatine. In the square, an archaic cistern (6th to 5th century B.C.).

From here we descend to the **House of Livia** or, according to others, of Augustus, a typical example of a patrician house of the last period of the Republic. The mural pictures in Pompeian style that still remain, are very interesting even though much damaged. Keeping to the left, we reach the **cryptoportico** built by Nero to unite the Palatine with the Domus Aurea. Then on the right we climb to the **Palace of the Flavii**, built by Domitian; it was designed by his architect, Rabirius.
It is formed on the left by a basilica, aula regia and lararium; in the centre by a peristilium. To the right is a triclinium where we see the ruins of the pavement and two Nymphaea, one of which is in good condition. Under the pavement there are traces of former constructions. Adjoining the palace was the **Domus Augustana**, a sumptuous edifice where his court lived. Near by, the **Paedagogium** or school for the imperial pages.

The **Stadium of Domitian** (175 yards long by 52 yds wide) is surrounded by fragments of porticoes, statues, fountains and, on one side, the niche of the imperial lodge. Then we come to the ruins of the **Baths of Septimius Severus**, a mass of constructions, then to the **Septizonium**, an imposing building whose remains were demolished by Sixtus V. From the Belvedere we enjoy a magnificent panorama.

At the foot of the hill, we see the elliptical form of the **CIRCUS MAXIMUS**, where the horse races took place. It was built under the kings, and more and more enlarged during the Republic and the Empire: under the reign of Constantine, it could contain more than 200.000 spectators. Chariot races, which were one of the favourite sports of the Roman people, took place here.

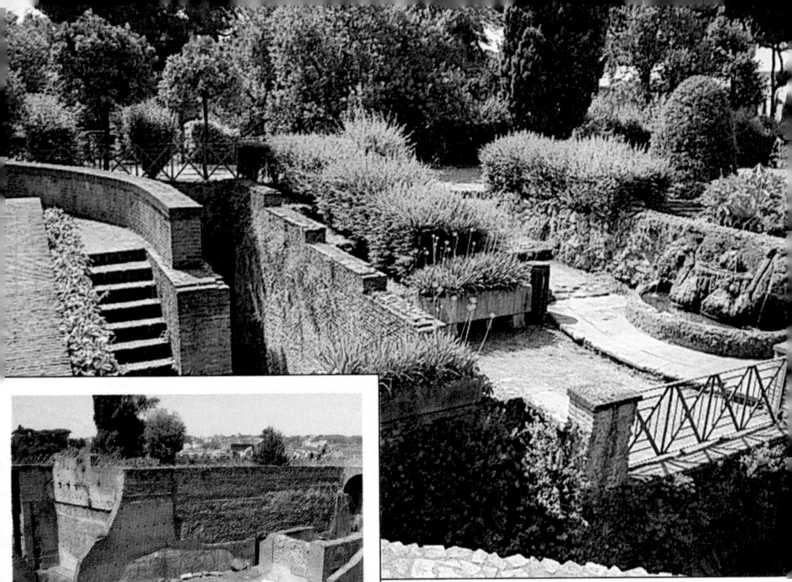

①

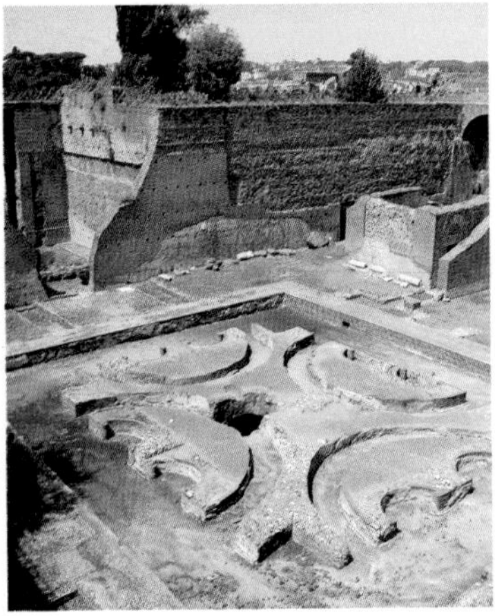

②

③

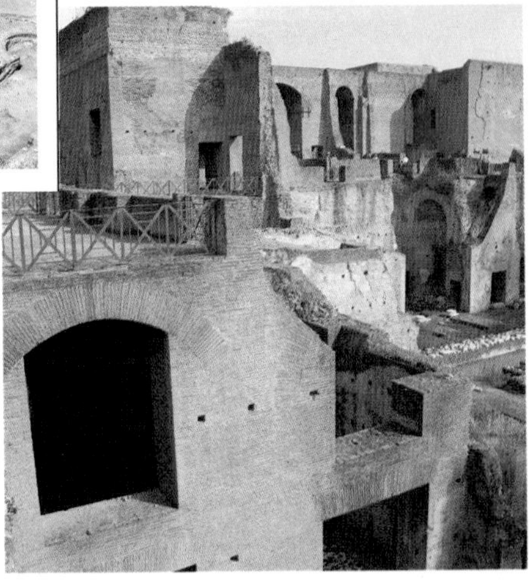

THE PALATINE

1) The Farnesian vegetable-gardens.

2) Courtyard of Augustana residence.

3) Rooms in Augustana residence.

4) Imperial Palaces.

④

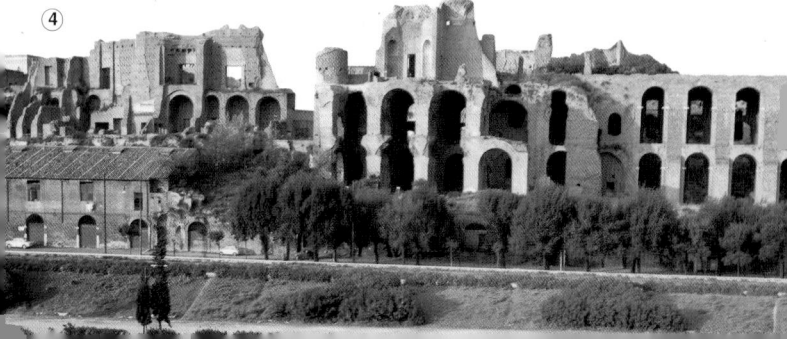

2nd itinerary
(see map)

From Piazza Venezia to the EUR

The Theatre of Marcellus · Tiber Island
St. Mary's in Cosmedin · The Pyramid · St. Paul's Basilica

The **Theatre of Marcellus** is the only antique theatre left in Rome. It is a fine edifice, erected by Augustus and dedicated to his sister Octavia's son, Marcellus, who died at the age of twenty-two greatly mourned and immortalized by Virgil's poem. Later on, this theatre served as a model for the construction of the Colosseum. We can still admire a part of the exterior curved wall with its double row of Doric and Ionic arches, surmounted on the upper part by the Savelli castle (later of the Orsini), erected by Baldassarre Peruzzi.

We come to the Tiber and see the characteristic **ISOLA TIBERINA** (Island in the Tiber). On the famous temple of Esculapius, the Greek god of medicine, once the centre for pilgrimages of sick persons, rises the church of **St. Bartholomew of the Island.**

The **Ponte Fabricio** (Quattro Capi) erected in 62 B.C. still almost intact today, and **Ponte Cestio** (46 B.C.) unite the island to the city.

The place occupied today by the Palatine Bridge was formerly the site of the **Ponte Sublicio**, noted for the legend of Horace Coclite.

On the other side we see the **Synagogue**, built in 1904 in Assyro-Babylonian style, with its grey cupola of aluminium. Behind lies the Ghetto, a neighbourhood where the Jews of Rome were segregated from the 6th century to the last century, and where today many Jews still cling tenaciously to their traditions.

Close to the street of the same name, are the remains of the **Portico of Ottavia** — the mother of Marcellus — which was built for her by her brother Augustus. The propylaea of the portico serves as the atrium of the church of **Sant'Angelo in Pescheria** (the name derives from the fish market which was once in front of it), founded in the 8th century. Let us return to the Via del Teatro di Marcello, where on

The area between the Colosseum and Circo Massimo in the days of Imperial Rome.

the site of the ancient Forum Boarium (the cattle market), today lies the characteristic **Piazza Bocca della Verità** against its interesting backdrop.

The **House of the Crescenzi** built in the 10th century by the powerful Crescenzi family, is an interesting piece of medieval construction, perhaps a fort guarding the river. Its decorations are formed by ancient fragments from several Roman buildings.

The temple called **Fortuna Virile** was not dedicated to this divinity but rather to Mater Matuta. It dates from the 1st century B.C. and is a fine example of the Greek-Italian architecture of Republican times.

Close by, is the beautiful **Circular Temple**, popularly known as the Temple of **Vesta**, perhaps because of its similarity with the temple of the same name in the Forum. However, it has not yet been possible to prove any of the attributions which have so far been suggested.

The **Church of San Giorgio in Velabro**, (called after the marshland of that name that once existed here) damaged and neglected over the years, was skilfully restored in 1926 to the sober forms of the 7th century, eliminating its baroque super-structures. The lovely bell-tower and the Ionic portico were built in the 12th century

The **Arch of the Argentari**, a curious monument covered with poor reliefs, was erected by the money-changers and shop-keepers of the Forum Boarium to Septimius Severus and Julia Domna, whose portraits are seen on the reliefs. Opposite is the entrance to the **Cloaca Massima** which once drained the water from the surrounding hills and emptied it into the Tiber. **The Arch of Janus** or ("Janus the four-faced") with its quadruple arch was built in Constantine's time as a covered passage in the centre of the cross-roads. It had a purely functional purpose: it served as a meeting place and shelter for local shopkeepers.

St. Mary's in Cosmedin, one of the gems of Medieval Rome, rises on the ruins of a temple, perhaps the temple of Ceres. The picturesque, austere interior gives us a clear idea of a primitive church (8th century). The **bell-tower** of Romanesque style, of the 12th century, is one of the most beautiful of its kind in Rome.

To the left of the portico is a marble mask called **Bocca della Verità** (mouth of truth); according to popular belief it was said that any one putting his hand in this mouth and swearing falsely, could not withdraw it.

The Synagogue.

After following the Aventine embankment of the Tiber and the Via Marmorata, we find ourselves at the Ostiense Gate, in front of the **Pyramid of Caius Cestius**, known in the Middle Ages as the tomb of Romulus. It was built during the last years of the Republic (1st century B.C.) to hold the ashes of Caius Cestius, Praetor, Tribune and Septemvirate of the Epulos, as the inscriptions recall.

Behind the Pyramid lies the **Non-Catholic Cemetery**, once known as the cemetery of the English where many of the foreigners who so loved Rome were laid to rest; from English poets such as Percy Bysshe Shelley and John Keats to the painter Henry Coleman, responsible for some of the most famous views of the Roman Campagna (countryside). About 2 kms. away on the Via Ostiense, (once in the heart of the countryside) rises the basilica of **ST. PAUL'S OUT-SIDE THE WALLS** (or the Ostiense Basilica), built over the burial place of the Apostle of the Gentiles. The building of the first place of worship over St. Paul's tomb has been attributed to the Emperor Constantine.

St. Mary's in Cosmedin.

*The Mouth
of Truth.*

A larger basilica was erected at the end of the 4th century. In the inscription on the mosaic of the triumphal arch, we read that Theodosius began it. Honorius finished it and under Leo I (440-461), Placidia restored and decorated it. This splendid basilica, one of the wonders of the world, was destroyed by fire in 1823. Rebuilt on the same foundations and according to the ancient design, the new Basilica was consecrated in 1854 by Pius IX.

The magnificent **four-sided portico** consisting of 150 columns with the majestic statue of St. Paul in the centre, was made by Giuglielmo Calderini between 1892 and 1928. The upper part of the **facade** covered in glittering mosaics by Filippo Agricola and Nicola Consoni, which represent **Christ giving his blessing,** the **Lamb of God, Saints** and **Prophets**. In the narthex, among other things is the bronze central door by Maraini, with its silver damascene work (1930).

The **interior of the basilica**, consisting of one nave and four aisles, is sumptuous and impressive: the eye is enchanted by the endless rows of columns, the mystic light from the double row of alabaster windows above them, the magnificent white and gold ceiling in Renaissance style, the shining marble pavement, reflecting the light and under the chancel arch the delightful canopy against the background of the gold mosaics of the apse. Between the windows and the columns, is a long sequence of medallions portraying the uninterrupted series of popes from St. Peter to the present day.

On the inner side of the facade, are six alabaster columns that were presented to Pope Gregory XVI after the fire by the Viceroy of Egypt, as a contribution to its rebuilding. The mosaics of the **chancel arch** date from the 5th century. The **canopy**, in Gothic style, raised on four columns of porphyry, admirable in harmony of line, is the unsurpassable work of Arnolfo di Cambio (13th century).

Under the **papal altar**, in the Confession, is the marble sarcophagus containing the glorious **relics of the Apostle**. In the transept on the right is the **altar of the Assumption** and on the left, the **Conversion of St. Paul**, in malachite and lapislazuli. To the right of the canopy, the famous **Easter Candlestick** in 12th century marble, the work of Nicolò dell'Angelo and Vassalletto, both Romans, seems a distant echo of the Roman columns.

In the «Chapel of the Blessed Sacrament», the first of the

four which line the transept and the only one which survived the fire, is the 14th century wooden crucifix which religious superstition maintains spoke to **St. Bridget**, who is shown in an attitude of contemplation in the first niche on the left. Her statue is by Stefano Maderno who worked in Rome in the first decade of the 17th century. The apse, whose reduced length makes the Basilica the shape of an Egyptian cross, is covered by an immense mosaic on a gold background made in the 13th century by Venetian artists. It survived the fire which spared this part of the Basilica. The **Cosmatesque cloister**, by Vassalletto, restored in 1907, revealing the ancient roof, must be considered one of the most noteworthy works of Roman marble sculptors, a real masterpiece for the elegant moulding, the richness and the elegance of its mosaics and its carvings.

Continuing towards the sea, after several kilometres the Via Ostiense and the Via del Mare run along the edge of the **E.U.R.**. This is an ultra-modern residential quarter planned at the end of the '30s as the site for a universal exhibition, which was unable to take place because of the outbreak of the 2nd World War. Although it has the typical dramatic features of fascist architecture, this neighbourhood's urban plan is pleasantly spacious and infinitely superior to other sprawling suburban developments which have sprung up over the last ten years in the outskirts of Rome.
Also worth noting, among the other buildings are the **Palazzo dei Congressi**, the **Palazzo della Civiltà e del Lavoro**, and the famous **Palazzo dello Sport** by Pier Luigi Nervi, with its bold architectural design, overlooking a lovely artificial lake which gives the area a particularly pleasant atmosphere.

The Basilica of St. Paul outside the Walls. In foreground the statue of St. Paul.

The Basilica of St. Paul outside the Walls - Inside.

The lake in EUR.

3rd itinerary
(see map)

From the Quirinal to
St. Mary Major's Basilica

The Quirinal · Via Veneto · Diocletian Baths

The **QUIRINAL** is so called from Quirinus, the Sabine name of the God Mars who was from remote times venerated on this hill, where, under Titus Tatius, the Sabines had emigrated. At the end of the Republic, Quirinus became identified with Romulus, son of Mars.

The immense **Quirinal Palace,** begun by Gregory XIII in 1547, was the Summer residence of the Popes until 1870. Then it became the residence of the King. Now the President of the Republic lives there.

Here we admire works by Maderno, Bernini, Guido Reni, Giulio Romano etc. The beautiful **Fountain,** (a granite basin which originally came from the Roman Forum) was moved to the square in 1818 by Raffaele Stern to support the obelisk from the Mausoleum of Augustus and the Statue of the heavenly twins, Castor and Pollux. On the right, the elegant and majestic **Palace of the Consulta,** by Fuga (1732-34). Walking down the Via del Quirinale, on the right stands the Church of **Sant'Andrea al Quirinale** (1658), Bernini's favorite work and to the far right, **San Carlino,** the work of Borromini: a very small church and cloister, but rich in grace and elegance. We have now reached the intersection of the **Quattro Fontane** (Four Fountains) with Porta Pia and the three obelisks of the Esquiline, the Quirinale and the Pincio in the background. The **four fountains** in each corner represent the Tiber and Aniene Rivers as well as the virtues of Loyalty and Strength.

Walking down Via delle Quattro Fontane, to the right, one can see the famous **Palazzo Barberini,** begun under Urban VIII based on **Maderno**'s design and completed by **Borromini** and **Bernini** in 1640. This Palace is the home of the **National Gallery of Ancient Art** which has recently been renovated and enlarged.

Among the many paintings exhibited, which range from the 12th to the 16th centuries, some are famous throughout the world such as **La Fornarina** by Raphael, **Christ and the**

Adulteress by Tintoretto, and **Narcissus** and **Judith Decapi-tating Holofernus** by Caravaggio. Inside the large hall of the Palace, one can admire the beautiful fresco in the vault by Pietro da Cortona depicting **The Triumph of Divine Providence** (1638).

At the end of the descent, one reaches **Piazza Barberini** with its highly original **Fountain of the Triton** by Bernini (1643). The piazza can be crossed diagonally to accede onto the famous **VIA VENETO.** At the beginning, to one's right, there is the gracious **Fountain of the Bees,** also the work of Bernini. Immediately after one can admire the Church of the Cappuccini with **Saint Michael** by Reni and **The Ecstasy of Saint Francis** by Domenichino. The macabre **Cemetery of the Cappuccini** is found underlying the Church.

Making a right onto Via Bissolati, one reaches Piazza San Bernardo with its **Fountain of Moses** commissioned by Six-tus V to Domenico Fontana who, overcoming various diffi-culties, succeeded in bringing the "Acqua Felice" to Rome from Colonna.

Piazza della Repubblica occupies the large area belonging to the Baths of Diocletian which we will discuss shortly. The **Fountain of the Naiads** dominates the piazza. The four smiling naiads are intertwined with just as many marine ani-mals in a play of sinuous and allusive shapes that are typi-cally liberty. The audacity of the figures sculpted by Mario Rutelli caused great controversy. Fearful of a scandal, the government postponed the inauguration of the fountain for some time until it was finally held on February 15, 1901. In the center of the fountain one can see the marble figure of the mythical fisherman **Glauco, struggling with a fish,** which Rutelli himself added to the composition in 1912.

The entire area is dominated by the colossal complex of the **BATHS OF DIOCLETIAN** which used to extend over a surface of thirteen acres, well beyond the majestic complex that still today we can admire between Piazza dei Cinque-cento and Piazza della Repubblica. In their entirety, the baths used to occupy the area among Piazza dei Cinque-cento, Via del Viminale, Via Torino, Via XX Settembre and Via Volturno.

The Emperor Diocletian had the baths built quickly between 298 and 306 A.D. in the level area of the Alta Semita, per-haps to favor the population of the Northern areas of Rome which were too distant from the Baths of Caracalla, built nearly one century before. Even though grandiose, the latter

The Fountain of the Triton by Bernini.

The Quirinal

Helicoidal staircase.

The Mascarino clock-tower.

could only hold 1,500 people while the Baths of Diocletian could contain over 3,000 people at one time.

The original plan of the baths can also clearly be seen in the **Church of Santa Maria degli Angeli and of the Martyrs** which Michelangelo built within the Roman complex respecting all the characteristics of his concepts and genius. The entrance into the basilica was to open in the direction of the present day Piazza dei Cinquecento, where the National Roman Museum is presently located, but in the 1700's, Luigi Vanvitelli altered the original project. Its present **entrance** was opened, formed by the façade of the calidarium of the baths. This change drastically reduced the impression of grandiosity obtained by Michelangelo thanks to the exceptional vastness of the entrance area he had originally chosen. The present **atrium** corresponds to the tepidarium of the baths. Its sober decorations faithfully preserve its original nature. The central part of the church, in the shape of a Greek cross favoured by Buonarroti, corresponds to the central hall of the baths. The **transversal nave**, which corresponds to Michelangelo's central nave, contains eight beautiful monolithic columns in red granite each one spectacular in size: 5 meters in circumference, 14 meters in height (taller than a four story building). Originally each column measured 16 meters in height, but Michelangelo was forced to raise the pavement by 2 meters in order to protect the church from the humidity. During the middle of the 1700's, Luigi Vanvitelli added the same amount of columns that were an imitation of granite and each with stucco capitals. The **apse** is also by Vanvitelli who cut into two halves the large pool or swimming area which had remained intact until then.

Behind the neighbouring Piazza dei Cinquecento, is the modern façade of the main railway station, **Stazione Termini** which was finished in 1950.

Founded in 1889, the **MUSEO NAZIONALE ROMANO** sits across a large piazza from Stazione Termini in what was once the Certosa of Santa Maria degli Angeli and the Baths of Diocletian, a stunning setting for one of the most precious archaeological collections in the world, made up of priceless relics found in Rome and Lazio in the last decades of the 19th century. The constant flow of archaeological finds necessitated the expansion of the museum, and two separate buildings, the nearby Palazzo Massimo alle Terme and Palazzo Altemps (at Piazza S. Apollinare, near Piazza Navona, see p. 99) have been recently renovated to hold a major portion of the collection. One of the most interesting parts at the **Baths of Diocletian** is the new arrangement of sarcophagi and the decorations of the Temple of Aurelian. Particularly suggestive is the interior of the Baths, including the **Aula Ottagona** (once a Planetarium), which after a recent restoration holds a 2nd century AD copy of a masterpiece by Praxiteles, the **Apollo Liceo**, and the splendid **Aphrodite of Cirene**, a 2nd century AD copy of a late-Hellenistic work. This statue was found in Cirenaica in 1913 and is made of pure Parian marble. The renovation of the baths did not alter the Great Cloister or **Cloister of Michelangelo**, attributed to the inimitable artist. Square in form, it is enclosed by a portico formed by one hundred arcades and one hundred columns. One of the most sumptuous cloisters in Rome, its walkways and central garden are richly adorned with statues and epigraphs.

PALAZZO MASSIMO ALLE TERME was built in 1887 by the architect Camillo Pistrucci for the Jesuit Massimiliano Massimo, and served as the seat for the College of Jesuits until 1960. In 1981, the Italian Government acquired the building and restored it as the second seat of the Museo Nazionale Romano. Dedicated to ancient art, Palazzo Massimo holds in its three floors the most significant works produced between the end of the Republican period (2nd-1st century BC) and the late-Imperial period (4th century AD), in addition to a few Greek works from the 5th century BC. It offers a complete picture of the political and economic life of ancient Rome.

The display on the ground floor is arranged in three galleries and eight rooms around a central courtyard. In the First Gallery are ten portraits from the late-Republican period. In the First Room, the visitor's attention is drawn to the marble statue of the so-called **General of Tivoli** (70 BC), found at Tivoli in the temple of Hercules Victor. In the Fifth Room is the **Augustus of Via Labicana**, in which the emperor appears in the clothing of the Pontifex Maximus, the saviour of the homeland. Several of the Greek sculptures in the Seventh Room come from the area of Sallust's Gardens (Rome's Ludovisi neighbourhood), once owned by the roman historian Sallust, and before that by Julius Caesar. The masterpiece of the room is the **Niobide** (440 BC). It represents a daughter of Niobe in the act of pulling an arrow out of her back, which Diana had shot. In the Eighth Room are copies of works by Greek sculptors made for Roman political figures who wanted to possess Greek works.

Via Vittorio Veneto is famous throughout the world for its elegance.

Piazza della Repubblica and the Fountain of the Naiads by Rutelli.

One of the four splendid nymphs of the Fountain of the Naiads.

The first floor contains two galleries and fourteen rooms, some containing portraits, reliefs and sarcophagi which are examples of the official ichnography of Roman art from the 1st to the 4th century AD. In the remaining rooms are pieces representing the rich bronze and marble statue production inspired by Greek sculpture of the 5th to 4th century BC. In the Fifth Room, for example, there are works which come from villas in Rome and Lazio, among them Hadrian's Villa and the Villas of Nero at Anzio and Subiaco.

The Sixth Room contains the notable **Apollo of the Tevere**, attributed to Fidia and found in the bottom of the river; two other noteworthy statues are the **Discobolo Lancellotti** and the **Discobolo di Castelporziano**.

In the Seventh Room is the large **statue of Dionysius**, a bronze work from Hadrian's period (2nd century AD) and a beautiful sculpture of the **Sleeping Hermaphrodite**, a copy of a Greek original (both from the 2nd century BC).

In the Second Gallery are fine feminine statue-portraits that date to the 3rd and 4th century AD: **Giulia Domna**, wife of Septimius Severus, **Plautilla**, wife of Caracalla, and **Salonina**, wife of Gallieno. The second floor holds **pictures**, **mosaics** and **stuccoes**, which demonstrate the luxury with which the villas and noble houses were decorated in Ancient Rome. Among the works are paintings of a garden from the Villa of Livia (wife of the Emperor Augustus) on the Via Flaminia; floor mosaics from the 2nd and 4th century AD; frescoes from the Villa of the Farnesina, along the Tiber, painted for the marriage of Agrippa and Julia in 19 AD; other mosaics, made of glass, shells and pumice, from the Nymphaeum of Anzio (1st and 2nd century AD) in the Villa of Nero; and floors from the Villa of Baccano on the Via Cassia (3rd century AD), which was probably owned by the Severi family.

Walking down Via Nazionale and turning to the left onto Via Depretis, one encounters the Palace of the Viminale where the offices of the Ministry of Interior are located. To the left, on Via del Viminale, we can also see the **Opera House**, built in the late eighteen hundreds and renovated by Piacentini (1926/28). Further down, we reach the **Tribuna of Santa Maria Maggiore**, erected on a high and majestic staircase which is masterfully built according to the slant of the ground. With its dynamic Baroque architecture (built in the late 600's by Flaminio Ponzio and Carlo Rinaldi), it represents one of the most beautiful apses in the world.

ST. MARY MAJOR is the greatest of many other churches dedicated to Our Lady; it is the only roman basilica which, in spite of several additional decorations, has preserved its original shape and character.

In the night of August 5th, 352, the Virgin appeared in a dream to the patriacian John and to Pope Liberius (352-366) commanding them to build a church on the spot where on the following day snow would fall. The miracle took place and the basilica was erected. This poetic legend is of late date and was recorded in the mediaeval mosaics that, much restored, may still be admired in the loggia of the vestibule. The basilica, also called "Liberiana", dates from the time of Sixtus III (432-440).

The **façade**, by Fuga (1743-1750), is pleasing. It has a porch with five portals, divided by pillars, adorned by columns and with a loggia above it, with three large arcades. Towering above it is the tallest belfry in Rome, built in Romanesque style. The **interior**, formed by a nave and two aisles, is a magnificent sight. At the end of a double row of columns, under the chancel arch, is the great **canopy** by Fuga, sustained by four precious columns of porphyry. The **ceiling**, by Julian Sangallo, was gilded according to tradition with the first gold brought from America. Along the architrave a series of thirty-six mosaics, reproducing scenes of the Old Testament is connected with those of the **chancel arch** showing scenes of the New Testament. All these mosaics are of the 5th century and are of exceptional importance and beauty. The pavement of the basilica is very fine cosmatesque work.

The **Confession** in front of the high altar was decorated in 1874 by Vespignani, who used the richest and rarest marbles. Behind the metal grill are the celebrated relics of the Crib, consisting of five pieces of the Manger in which the Christ-child was placed at his birth, enclosed in a silver urn designed by Valadier. Opposite is the large kneeling **Statue of Pius IX**, by Jacometti.

The **High altar** under the great canopy is the sarcophagus containing the bones of St. Matthew, the Evangelist. In the apse with ogival windows we admire the **Triumph of Mary**, a fine mosaic by I. Turriti (1295).

In the first chapel is the Baptistery by the architect Flaminio Ponzio. The porphyry **Baptismal font** is by Valadier. At the altar is the **Assumption**, a basrelief by Bernini.

The Basilica of St. Marie Major was erected by Sisto III. ➡

The Basilica of St. Marie Major - The Apse with the precious mosaic by Torriti (1295).

The Canopy and the Confessional of the Basilica of St. Marie Major.

The **Sistine chapel** was constructed by the great architect Domenico Fontana (born at Como in 1543, died at Naples in 1607), by order of Cardinal Felice Peretti, who wanted to raise a monument in gratitude to Pius V who had made him cardinal. Over the altar of the Holy Sacrament is the **Tabernacle** upheld by four gilded bronze angels, designed by Ricci. The two monumental **Tombs of Sixtus V** and **Pius V** have been compared to the ancient triumphal arches for their decorative reliefs which seem, by the effect of light and chiaroscuro, almost as if they were painted. They represent episodes of the lives of the two Popes.

Sixtus V did many memorable things in the five years of his pontificate (1586-1590). Gregory XIII had left the Papal States in a terrible condition. Thousands of bandits infested the land and the new Pope in a short time re-established order.

He also improved financial conditions and spent enormous sums of money to beautify Rome. He finished the dome of St. Peter's, erected the Lateran Loggia and the Lateran Palace, raised obelisks, opened new streets, brought the Acqua Felice to Rome, tried to drain the Pontine marshes: he created Sixtine Rome. Great sovereign in an era of great sovereigns, he showed in all his actions a·highly original and eminently practical mind. Pius V promoted the Christian League that led to the great battle of Lepanto (October 7th, 1571), the crucial battle for Christian civilization.

At the end of the right aisle, the **Tomb of Cardinal Consalvo Rodriguez**, by Giovanni di Cosma (1299), perhaps the finest monument in this basilica, an example of that renaissance in art that began with the Cosmati and ended with the great artist Cavallini (13th century).

At the end, on the left, the **Tomb of the Merlini Family**, by Borromini.

In front of the Sistine Chapel is the **Paolina** (or Borghese) **Chapel**, erected for Paul V (Borghese) by Flaminio Ponzio, who copied the design of Fontana for the Sixtine chapel. It is the richest, most beautiful chapel in Rome. All the splendour of this basilica is condensed in this patrician chapel: bronzes and frescoes gleam from the walls and from the fantastic ceiling. There are **frescoes** by Guido Reni, Cav. d'Arpino, Cigoli and others, all designed for the apotheosis of the Virgin. Above the high altar of agate and lapslazuli is one of Rome's greatest treasures, the miraculous picture of the **Madonna and Child** which the people attributed to

St. Luke the Evangelist. On either side of the chapel, are the **tombs of Pope Paul V and Pope Clement VIII**, the work of Flaminio Ponzio in the early 17th century.

In the same aisle, it is worth noticing the **Sforza Chapel**, built by Giacomo Della Porta (1564) to a design attributed to Michelangelo.

In front of the church stands a beautiful **Corinthian column** erected here by Paul V who had it removed from the basilica of Constantine in the Forum.

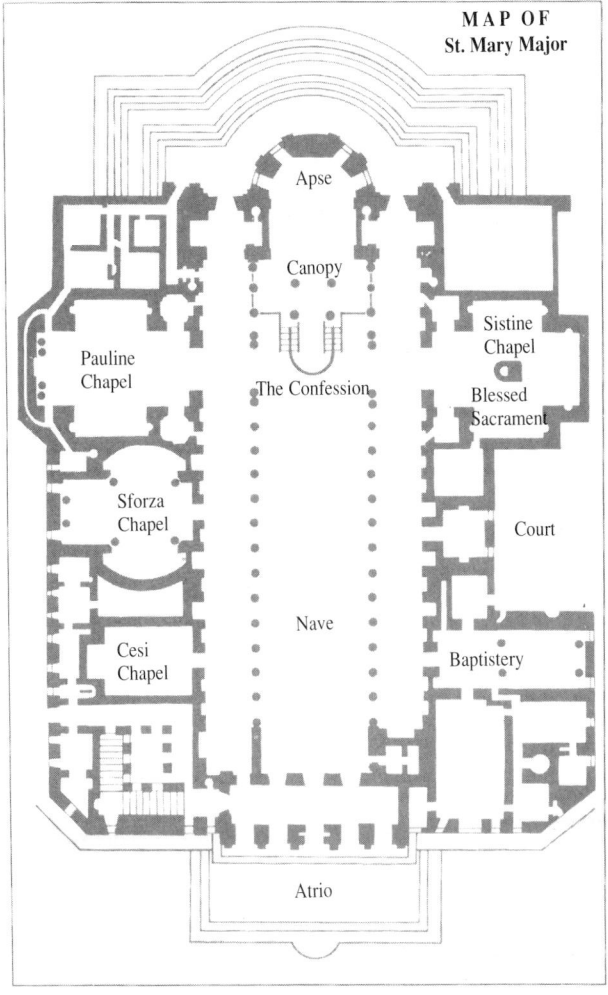

4th itinerary
(see map)

From Piazza Venezia to
St. Lawrence outside the Walls

*St. Peter in Chains · Nero's Golden House · St. Clement
The Basilica of St. John in the Lateran*

From the Via dei Fori Imperiali, we turn into Via Cavour, where, on the left, stands the medieval **Tower of the Conti**. Further along, we come to the Staircase of St. Francis of Paola, dominated by the **House of the Borgia** that was built over an arch, under which passes the upper part of the staircase leading to S. Pietro in Vincoli. The house and place recall scenes of crime and blood. Here the Duke of Candia was killed in the night of June 14th, 1497. Here, in the since vanished Vico Scellerato. Tullia in her coach purposely ran over the dead body of her father, King Servius Tullius.

On a characteristic isolated small square, which is easily reached through Via Cavour, it is founded another Basilica, **SAINT PETER IN CHAINS**, which is object of a particular veneration for many reasons. So this Basilica, in fact, has very ancient origins, and is dedicated to a precious relics dating back to the first times of the Christianity.

In fact it was founded in the V Century for which of the Empress Eudossia in the place of another pre-existent Basilica so that the chains (*vinculi* in latin) of Saint Peter discovered in Jerusalem would be kept. Also in this case, the long centuries of history have left their mark on the original construction, deeply altering the features, especially during the reconstruction of the eighteenth Century of Francesco Fontana.

On the facade it is of considerable interest, mostly, **the portico** made by an elegant architect (the attribution of its making wavers between Baccio Pontelli and Meo del Caprino) on wish of Cardinal Giuliano della Rovere, the future bellicose Julius II, who ordered Michelangelo the construction of his own grave. The most famous masterpiece was part of this monument, **the MOSES**, that most of the visitors go to the venerable Basilica in order to admire it.

The statue had to form the main figure of the grandiose Mausoleum that could not be realised in its primary majes-

Mosé by Michelangelo.

tic conception. This was one of the most painful torments for the artist who, at the end, after many vicissitudes succeeded in realising only its reduction in poor dimensions, placed on the right wing of the transept.

Nevertheless, although the monument is quite far from being the superb dream of the sculptor-architect, in which as many forty statues had to find place (which had to be formed by forty statues), the powerful figure of the biblic prophet is still, on good right, among the figurative images of the Western art the most impressive in the spirit of any visitor even in its most faded reproduction. Moses is represented in an extremely simple position, still spreading a feeling of majesty beyond the words: it is impossible not to recognise in him a leader so much stronger and secure of himself as his power derives from the divine investiture, from the amazing mystery of the biblic episode of Sinai.

Omitting a minute illustration of the other, although extremely worthy, masterpieces contained in the Basilica, we recall only the **golden bronze urn** of the XIX century placed in the Confession, underneath the High Altar, in which there are saved the **Chains of Saint Peter**. Object of deep veneration are the relics of the seven Maccabei Brothers, kept in a burial paleochristian sarcophagus with episodes of the New Testament, settled in the crypt.

In the **COLLE OPPIO** is the access to the celebrated **Domus Aurea** of Nero, an imposing, fantastic group of buildings that extended from the Palatine to the Esquiline, submerged in the greenery of a countryside recreated within the city occupying an extensive area. However, of so many marvels, almost everything disappeared instantly after the death of Nero. His successors wanted to eradicate the slightest memory of these achievements, whose luxury had aroused passionate hatred in Roman hearts. This was the site of the central pavilion, ruined in 104 by a terrible fire.

Over it were built the foundations for the construction of the **Baths of Trajan**, of which only a few ruins remain.

The grottoes underneath, once believed to belong to the **Baths of Titus**, were explored by artists of the Renaissance who learned here a special decorative style purposely called "grotesque". Here the famous Laocoon was found, and also the enormous porphyry vase (see Vatican Museum) in which, Poppea is supposed to have bathed in the milk of one hundred she-asses.

Even in the cold, concise terms of the historian Suetonius,

Nero's Golden House (Domus Aurea) appears to us like an enchantment from the *Arabian Nights*. It consisted in countless pavillons scattered over an immense park, and was adorned with works of art taken from cities and temples in Greece, while gold and precious stones embellished the walls. Today the vast imposing underground halls can barely hint at such magnificence.

We cannot, of course, describe them fully; we shall only mention the **"crypto-portico"** which isolated the north part of the construction from the hill behind; the names of the Renaissance artists who first went there are carved on the ceiling. It is also worth noticing the great rectangular **nymphaeum**, culminating in an imposing apse, whose rich decorations have been restored and are clearly visible today. The **room with the golden vault** decorated with the most delicate plaster work; the **octagonal room**, covered by a vaulted pavilion with a central opening. According to the historian Suetonius, the vault slowly rotated, thanks to a special mechanism, while from appropriate flower-shaped holes in laminate of ivory, flower petals and perfumes showered down upon the guests.

The **basilica of ST. CLEMENT**, mentioned by St. Jerome in the 4th century, is one of the most interesting in Rome from an artistic and archeological point of view. It was almost buried under the enormous quantity of debris accumulated in that zone after the terrible fire caused by the Normans in 1084, but was rebuilt in the 12th century by Paschal II on a higher level. The new basilica was built in the original form with all the architectural elements it was possible to save, so that it remains, in spite of restorations and modification of more recent date, a rare example of a typical early Christian basilica.

It was not possible to preserve its width, since the new building had to exclude the whole area of the aisle beneath on the right, whose foundations were too damaged. In fact embedded within the outer wall of the upper church, are the arches of the colonnade which in the lower basilica divided the right hand aisle from the large central nave. It was on this spot that the new right hand aisle was also built as well as the reduced central nave. It was therefore made narrower than the left hand aisle, the only one of the three which corresponds exactly with the one beneath. Two rows of columns divide the three aisles, interspersed

The Holy Staircase - The Sancta Sanctorum.

St. Peter in Chains. The famous chains with whic. St. Peter was imprisoned

with pilasters. Each of the columns is different. They were certainly recovered from the remains of many buildings ruined in the fire we have already mentioned. The most typical elements of the upper basilica are the **protiro** (or entrance porch) and within, the "schola cantorum" whose enclosure, with plutei and transennae, belonged to the ancient basilica, while the ambos and the twisted column of the candelabra are of the 12th century. The tabernacle and the episcopal seat in the centre of the typical semi-circular choir stalls for the clergy which run along the apse, are from the same period. But the glory of this Basilica are the mosaics on the apse which, in a prodigious synthesis of Christian and pagan figurative elements, portray the **Scene of the Redemption**. It is a masterpiece of the 12th century Roman school.

Besides the underground basilica, brought to light during the excavations which took place in the last century, and other Imperial and Republican constructions including a "Mithraeum", this place is also of extraordinary interest to archeologists.

There are notable works of art of the Renaissance in this basilica. In the first chapel of the left aisle, we admire the famous frescoes of Masolino da Panicale (1431), formerly attributed to Masaccio. In the centre to the left. St. Christopher; on the central wall, a dramatic Crucifixion; on the later walls, to the right, episodes from the life of St. Ambrose, and St. Catherine, to the left. On the altar a Madonna, by Sassoferrato.

Here we are on the square of St. John in the Lateran. In front of the Basilica's side facade, the **obelisk of the Lateran** rises, the highest of the thirteen which were erected in the squares of Rome. It was made in 1449 B.C. by Totmes III and his son Totmes IV of the XVIII dinasty of the Pharaohs and transported in the 4th century to Rome, where it was set up in the Circus Maximus. Sixtus V had it re-erected here by Fontana (1588).

The **LATERAN** was the residence of the Popes up to 1309 i.e. until they moved from Rome to Avignon. Their palace, the "Patriarchium", was pulled down in 1596 by Domenico Fontana by command of Pope Sixtus V, who ordered the present one to be built.

On the right of the square is the **Baptistery**. It was erected by the Emperor Constantine where, according to an erroneous tradition, he had been christened by Saint Silvester. Later on, it was rebuilt by order of Sixtus III (432-440) and afterwards several popes had it restored. It is an octagonal structure. Eight columns of porphyry sustain the cornice and another eight of marble the dome.

To the left of the square is the **Scala Santa**. According to tradition it is the same flight of marble steps which Jesus ascended in the house of Pilate; it was brought to Rome by the pious Empress Helena. The twenty-eight steps may only be ascended kneeling. At the top of the stairs is the private chapel of the Popes which formed a part of old Patriarchium, called the "Sancta Sanctorum", richly decorated by the Cosmati in 1278. At the sides of the staircase are two splendid groups by Jacometti: the "Kiss of Judas" and "Pilate showing Christ to the people" (1854).

ST. JOHN IN THE LATERAN is the Cathedral of Rome, the mother of all churches in Rome and in the world. Founded by Constantine and called the "Basilica of the Saviour" during the time of Silvester (314-335) it has been destroyed and rebuilt many times. The actual basilica dates from the 17th century.

The imposing facade in travertine was constructed in 1735 by Alexander Galilei, who used all his architectural ability on the portico. To the left we see a Statue of Constantine which was found at the Quirinal; a poor statue, showing the decadence of art at that time. The bronze doors were taken from the Curia in the Forum, by Alexander VII (1655-1667).

The inside, with its five aisles, retains little of the ancient mediaeval basilica; the same antique columns of granite were covered by pilasters by Borromini in the course of the radical reconstruction which was carried out in the mid-17th century. Against the new pilasters, the artist arranged twelve imposing **tabernacles** each with two ancient green marble columns, which came from the old Basilica. The **statues of the Apostles** all round the nave, are of the Bernini school. The basreliefs are among the most important works of Algardi (1603-54). The ceiling is the superb work of F. Boulanger and Vico di Raffaele. The pavement is cosmatesque. Underneath it were found notable remains of ancient constructions.

The **lateral aisles** were totally rebuilt by Borromini, with a rhythmic succession of arches in the intermediae aisles

The Basilica of St. John in Lateran.

The Basilica of St. John in Lateran - The Cloister.

The Basilica of St. John in Lateran - Inside.

and architraves in the outer aisles, which give it a new spirit, original and vigorous.

The many funeral monuments already in existance were re-organized in baroque aediculae by Borromini, who had no qualms about dismantling them when he felt it was necessary, with a decisiveness which would cause a scandal today.

By the first pillar, on the side of the right intermediate aisle, is a part of a large fresco, under glass, that Giotto painted for Cardinal Stefaneschi after the first Jubilee of 1300, **Boniface VIII proclaiming the Jubilee.**

At the next pillar the **Tomb of Silvester II** (999-1003) the most learned man of his time. He travelled to collect manuscripts of ancient authors. He was the first to proclaim the necessity of the Crusades to free Jerusalem. At the third pillar, is **the monument to Alexander III** (1159-1181) who led the fight against Frederic Barbarossa (1123-1190). In 1166 the Emperor besieged the Vatican, after devastating various territories of Italy. The Pope mobilized the Lombardy League against him, an alliance of Italian municipalities. They erected the fortress of Alessandria, which received this name in honour of the Pope. After the Italian victory in Legnano, negotiations began which ended with the Peace Treaty of Venice, where the proud Emperor knelt to kiss the Pope's foot. In the centre of the transept, is the **Papal Altar**, surmounted by a canopy supported by four columns, built in 1367 by Urban V (1362-1370). Beneath it, can be seen a bronze plaque: the splendid work of Simone, Donatello's brother; on this is sculpted the recumbent figure of **Martin V** (1417-1431) remembered in the inscription as "temporum suorum felicitas" (the happiness of his times).

To the right of the tribune, is the **Monument to Innocent III** (1198-1216) designed by Lucchetti by order of Leo XIII who had his remains brought here from the cathedral of Perugia. Innocent III, a learned man of great ability, was elected Pope at a time when Europe was in a state of ruin. In this basilica he proclaimed the Fifth Crusade; here the twelfth Ecumenical Council was held, the fourth of the Lateran, that most brilliant and widely attended meeting that marked another culminating point in papal power.

Leo XIII ordered the architect Vespignani to extend the apse. The transfer of the * **Mosaic of the Redeemer** was ably executed and this venerable work was also restored.

It dates back to the first building of the Basilica (4th century) and was restored for the first time in 1291 almost a thousand years later, by Jacopo Torriti and Jacopo da Camerino. High up, it shows the smiling face of the Redeemer giving his blessing, which appeared, according to legend, on the apse of the Basilica as soon as it was built, thus sanctioning the sublime rite with his divine presence. The **Papal throne** below, which in this Basilica, the Cathedral of Rome, is also the bishops' throne, is made of precious marbles studded with dazzling mosaics.

To the left of the Tribune, the splendid **Monument to Leo XIII**, noble work of Tadolini. Leo XIII, one of the greatest modern Popes, was buried here in October 1924. In this monument, Tadolini combined the Renaissance style with the modern. The statue on the left, a workman, reminds us of the encyclical "Rerum Novarum" (1891), called the Magna Charta of Christian Sociology, in which Leo established the reciprocal relations between workers and employers in the practice of justice and love.

The **Altar of the Sacrament** to the left of the transept was designed by Olivieri at the time of Clement VIII (1592-1605). The four bronze columns, the only ones of the kind known, were taken from the Capitol by the Emperor Constantine. Through a door between the left hand aisle and the transept one goes out into the airy **cloister**, the work of famous Roman marble workers of the 13th century, the Vasallettos. It has remained almost intact, and though it is made out of a combination of extremely varied elements, it gives a harmonious impression of unity.

Not far off rises the Basilica of the **HOLY CROSS IN JERUSALEM** (or Sessoriana or Eleniana Basilica). It is thought to have been built, or rather, to have been adapted from the Sessorian palace, in the beginning of the 4th century, by the Mother of Constantine, St. Helena, who placed a **Relic of the Holy Cross** there together with others found by her at Jerusalem. It has often been restored and in 1743 it was almost entirely rebuilt by order of Benedict XIV. The facade, standing in the centre of the plain walls of the Cistercian monastery, is characterized by a curved and sinuous outline. The atrium is particularly original, built to an oval design with the entrance on the lesser curve and covered by a dome which is also oval. The 13th century bell tower is still standing. The interior has a nave and two aisles. In the apse is a fresco by Antoniazzo Romano, the

The Basilica of Holy Cross in Jerusalem.

Discovery of the Holy Cross. The **Chapel of Relics** is the work of the architect Di Fausto (1930). In the crypt is a marvellous mosaic by Melozzo da Forlì. The **Statue of St. Helena**, except for the head and the hands, is a reproduction of the Juno Vaticana.

Nearby rises the **Porta Maggiore**, more imposing than all the gates of Rome. It is a monumental arch with two vaults constructed at the time of Claudius. The inscription records the construction of Claudius' aqueduct and the restorations by Vespasian and Titus.

The fifth patriarchal basilica **S. LORENZO FUORI LE MURA** (St. Lawrence outside the walls), was originally erected by Constantine; after the sack by Alaric and the Goths, Pelagius II rebuilt it during 579-590. The Longobards damaged it further, and Hadrian I (722-795), or according to others, Honorius III (1216-26) restored it in such a way that the old Constantinian part of the basilica became the presbitery of the new one; the original entrance was on the opposite side.

In the 13th century portico by Vassalletto there are six Ionic columns; two Roman **Lions** flank the portal. On the right, a block of stone commemorates the unfortunate bombardment of July 19, 1943, after which a large part of the Basilica had to be rebuilt. The restoration which was completed in 1949, left the three aisles their original design. There is a row of twenty-two columns of granite and cipollino marble which were taken from ancient monuments. On the right of the central door of the church is a Roman sarcophagus decorated with a finely carved scene of a nuptial ceremony. It was adapted as **a Tomb for Cardinal Fieschi**, nephew of Innocent IV, who died in 1256. The two large amboes are of the Cosmati epoch. The floor is also cosmatesque. A large hole opened by the bombardment uncovered traces of the apse of the Basilica of Constantine's time.

5th itinerary
(see map)

From Piazza Venezia to Trastevere

*Torre Argentina
Campo de' Fiori · The Janiculum*

The **Fountain of the Tortoises** in the small Piazza Mattei, is the most charming in Rome. Its beauty and its fine lines gave birth to the legend that this artistic jewel of the late 16th century was designed by Raphael; in reality, it is the work of Landini (1585).

Four republican temples not impressive in size but interesting and very ancient, have come to light in the monumental zone of largo Torre Argentina. Close by is the Argentina Theatre where, in 1816, Rossini presented his "Barber of Seville" for the first time. Hissed at the first evening, it was a triumphant success on the second performance.

S. Andrea della Valle was built, on the design of C. Maderno, from 1591 to 1650. The dome, the highest in Rome after St. Peter's, is also one of the finest. The façade of travertine is an impressive work by Rainaldi.

The interior forms a Latin cross. The ample nave, wide, beautiful and full of light, the large side chapels, the apse, the ceiling and dome all combine to give an impression of splendour and solemnity. The first chapel on the right (Ginnetti-Lancellotti) is by C. Fontana. The second (Strozzi) is the superb work of G. della Porta after the design of Michelangelo. His architecture is at once solemn and austere. On the altar, the **Pietà** between **Lea and Rachel**, a perfect reproduction in bronze of Michelangelo's work. The four tombs in black marble belong to members of the Strozzi family. Two magnificent candelabra ornament the entrance. Towards the end of the nave, high up the Tombs of Two Piccolomini Popes: on the left, Pius II; on the right, Pius III. In the presbytery, stuccoes by Algardi and frescoes by Domenichino, reproduce scenes of the life of St. Andrew. In the dome, the **Glory of Paradise**, by Lanfranco; in the consoles, the Evangelists, noble figures by Domenichino.

The **Campo de' Fiori** is the place where for a long time capital punishments took place. Here on February 17th 1600, the philosopher **Giordano Bruno**, who escaped punishment in Switzerland, Bohemia and England, was burned as an heretic. The monument is the fine work of Ettore Ferrari (1887). The lively market makes this square typical of old Rome even today.

The superb **Farnese Palace**, in the square of the same name, was begun under Paul III on designs by Sangallo the younger and finished under the direction of Michelangelo, to whom we owe the marvellous cornice, the central window of the façade and part of the courtyard. Annibale Caracci and his pupils worked for more than eight years to decorate it. This majestic and magnificent national monument was bought in 1908 by France that by then had established its Embassy to the Quirinal there.

And now, after crossing the Ponte Amedeo di Savoia, we go up to the **JANICULUM**, from where there is a most varied and attractive view of the Eternal City. At the end of the slope of Sant'Onofrio we enter the villa, where the beautiful, "Passeggiata of the Gianicolo" running all round the hill, begins.
On the right, in the **Church of St. Onophrius**, stands the Monument to Torquato Tasso, a work by De Fabris, erected by order of Pope Pius IX two and a half centuries after the poet's death.
In the adjoining convent, Tasso lived for some time waiting for the day of his coronation as a poet at the Capitol. But on April 25th, 1595, on the eve of his triumph, he died. Proceeding along the slope, amid a group of cypresses we come across the historical ruin of **Tasso's oak**, beneath which the poet loved to sit in the shade and where San Filippo Neri gathered many young boys in order to teach them by amusing them.
Still further, on the left, there is the 16th century **Lante Pavillon** and on the right we see the **Monument to Anita Garibaldi**, a splendid work by M. Rutelli (1932). Still further we reach the large terrace of the Gianicolo on which stands the **Monument to Giuseppe Garibaldi**, a work by E. Gallori (1895).
It is from this terrace that one has the most famous view of the city.
Over the undulating sea of roofs, the numerous domes of

Fountain of the Tortoises.

Rome are silhouetted against the distant backdrop of an amphitheatre of mountains, while the Tiber with its meanders determines the city's unmistakable shape. The Passeggiata Gianicolense ends in the beautiful avenue bordered by the busts of the patriots of the Roman Republic (1849). On the right of the exit, we see the **Fontana Paolina**, the most splendid fountain in Rome, made by G. Fontana and C. Maderno, erected in 1611 by Paul V who wished to restore the aqueduct constructed by Trajan in the year 109 in order to carry the water from the Bracciano Lake

The Basilica of St. Mary in Trastevere .

*Tempietto by Bramante
of St. Peter in Montorio.*

to Rome. The vast semicircular basin was added in 1690
by Carlo Fontana.
Further down, on the left, we come to the church of **San
Pietro in Montorio** where Beatrice Cenci (1577-1599) famous for her tragic history, was buried. She was arrested
with other members of her family and on September 11th,
1599 they were all executed.
The famous Renaissance architect Bramante built his glorious **Tempietto** in the court-yard of the convent, on the spot
where, according to tradition, St. Peter was crucified.

Following the Via Garibaldi, down the hill from the Janiculum one reaches **Trastevere,** the "heart of Rome" and a
very popular district which we hope will keep its character
in spite of the changes due to a certain internationalization
of this famous part of the city. A detailed visit cannot be
included in this itinerary due to an obvious lack of space.
However, we advise you to end this fascinating walk by
wandering through the streets in Trastevere, where you can
still get a feeling of the most genuine atmosphere of the
city. We shall mention only in passing the oldest basilica
of Rome, **St. Mary's in Trastevere** which is to be found
in the square of the same name. Founded in 221 by St.
Calixtus, and finished by St. Julius (341) it was rebuilt in
the 12th century by Innocent II.
The **facade** was decorated in the same century with mosaics
and frescoes, which were later restored by P. Cavallini. Clement XI, in the 18th century, had the portico built by Carlo
Fontana, while Pius IX (1870) ordered various restorations.
Next to the facade, there is a beautiful 12th century
romanesque bell-tower, and high up an aedicula, with a
Madonna and Child in mosaics.

6th itinerary
(see map)

From Piazza Venezia to Foro Italico

Via del Corso · The Trevi Fountain
Trinità dei Monti · Villa and Gallery Borghese

The **VIA DEL CORSO** is the principal, most central, and most typical of the old Roman streets. At one end of its narrow but imposingly straight line, nearly a mile long, is the obelisk of the Piazza del Popolo; at the other end, the "Vittoriano". It is bordered with many papal and princely palaces (Salviati, Odescalchi, Sciarra, Marignoli, on the right; Bonaparte, Doria, Chigi, Fiano, Ruspoli, Rondanini, on the left). The name Corso (race, derived from the special horse races that took place there up to the past century: it replaced the ancient "via Lata".

Let us now walk towards the Piazza del Popolo. The first palace we see on the left, the corner palace, is that of **Bonaparte**, where Letitia, mother of Napoleon I, lived and died. Next comes the **Doria-Pamphili** palace, one of the most splendid of papal Rome. The Doria Gallery is on the first floor. It is reached by the entrance at the back of the palace, and contains a wealth of 16th and 17th paintings, including the **portrait of Innocent X**, by the Spanish painter Velasquez: few portraits can compare with this, where the accomplished artist reveals all his talents. We come next to the beautiful façade of **Santa Maria in Via Lata** by Pietro da Cortona. Further on the right, the **Church of St. Marcellus** with a bizarre baroque façade. Following the Via del Caravita on the left, we reach the **Church of St. Ignatius**, of Jesuit-baroque style. The stupendous fresco on the ceiling, the "Triumph of St. Ignatius" is in admirable perspective. A round marble slab on the pavement indicates the place to stand to get the best view. In the right transept, under the altar, is the Body of St. Louis Gonzaga.

In the adjacent Piazza di Pietra is the **Temple of Hadrian** (so-called Temple of Neptune). One of its sides, with Corinthian columns, has been beautifully restored. The Stock Exchange now occupies one of its halls.

Trevi Fountain - Aerial view.

To the right fo the Via del Corso, in the Via delle Muratte, is the most sumptuous fountain in Rome.

The **FONTANA DI TREVI** is not only celebrated for its excellent water but for the legend that whoever drinks it or throws a coin in the fountain, will assure his return to Rome. It is the façade of a large palace decorated with statues and bas-reliefs on heaps of rocks: the water gushes from every part. It was Agrippa who brought the Virgin Water to Rome by means of an aqueduct. The fountain was built by the architect Salvi (1735) in the time of Clement XII, and decorated by several artists of Bernini's school. It is said that the soldiers of Agrippa, looking for water in the via Collatina in the country, met a maiden who showed them the source of this pure water, which was hence called Virgin Water. The bas-relief on the right represents this event; that on the left shows Agrippa explaining to Augustus the plan to bring this water to Rome.
A thorough restoration has recently been completed, (1991), which has given it back all its original splendour.
Almost half way down of the Corso is the **Piazza Colonna**, with the Column of Marcus Aurelius. After the death of the Emperor-Philosopher. the Senate erected a temple and a column in his honour. The column was surmounted by a bronze statue of the Emperor.
On the square is the **Chigi Palace**, the Prime Minister's Office. On the opposite side of the Corso is the Colonna Gallery. The **Montecitorio Palace** on the square close by with the same name is the headquarters of the Chamber of Deputies: the old section, Innocent's Palace, was built by Bernini, the newest part was built by Basile, (1650-1694). Nearby, on the left of the Via del Corso is the **Church of St. Lawrence in Lucina** with a portico and a bell-tower of the 12th century. At the high altar, the famous **Crucifixion** by Guido Reni.

Continuing, we come to the Largo Goldoni. From here, by the Via Condotti, we reach the **PIAZZA DI SPAGNA**. The first thing that strikes one is the charming, monumental **flight of steps** (1772) whose sinuous lines harmoniously follow the slope of the hill. At its feet is the graceful **Fountain of the Little Boat** by P. Bernini. On the right, in the next square, Piazza Mignanelli, is the **column of the Immaculate Conception**, a monument erected to commemorate the proclamation of the Dogma (1856).

At the top of the Spanish steps is the Church of the **TRINI-TÀ DEI MONTI**, with its two cupolas (1495), and in front of its facade is an obelisk, which was taken from the Sallustian gardens in 1789.

Inside the church, the masterpiece of Daniele da Volterra, the famous fresco of the Descent from the Cross.

Returning to the Via del Corso, we see to our left, the baroque church of **St. Charles in the Corso**. At the main altar the Glory of St. Ambrose and St. Charles by Maratta. The heart of St. Charles is kept here in a rich reliquary. Going to the back of the church we admire the outside of the magnificent tribune. In the centre of the Piazza Augusto Imperatore is the **Mausoleum of Augustus**. Built as a tomb for the Emperor and his family one century before Hadrian, the monument has known some very different uses over the centuries: transformed into a fort in the 12th century by the Colonna family, later dismantled and used as a marble quarry, it was finally adapted for use as a concert hall (noted for its fine acoustics) and served this purpose until 1936.

In the Via Ripetta is the **Ara Pacis Augustae**, a historic monument built under Emperor Augustus in the year B.C. 13 to celebrate the peace re-established all over the Roman world.

In the last section of the Via del Corso, at number 20, is the German **Goethe Museum**, arranged in the house where the great poet lived during his intense stay in Rome.

PIAZZA DEL POPOLO was designed by Valadier at the turn of the century. It is an enormous square, architecturally superb and perfectly symetrical. In the centre stands the city's second **obelisk**, which was brought to Rome by Augustus, and re-erected here by Fontana under Sixtus V (1589).

According to the legend, in the early middle ages Nero's spirit haunted this place where his ashes had been deposited in the Domitian family's tomb. This is why the people destroyed the Mausoleum and built a church there, **S. MARIA DEL POPOLO**, one of the most interesting in Rome. It was probably built in the 11th century, but it was completely reconstructed in the early Renaissance.

Among the many works of art to be seen here are: Adoration of the Child, by Pinturicchio on the altar of the first chapel on the right; a Tabernacle by Andrea Bregno, in

The romantic lake in Villa Borghese Park .

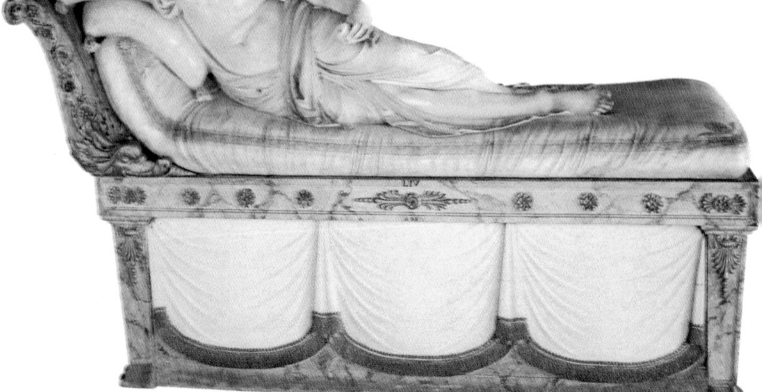

*The statue of Paolina Borghese
by Canova.*

the Sacristy; two monuments by Sansovino: to Cardinal della Rovere, on the right, and to Cardinal Sforza, on the left of the high altar. On the ceiling, the Coronation of the Virgin and other frescoes by Pinturicchio; two masterpieces by Caravaggio: **Saul on the road to Damascus**, on one side, the **Crucifixion of St. Peter**, on the other, in a chapel of the transept on the left.

The Chigi chapel, the second in the left aisle, was designed by Raphael; it is a real jewel of the Renaissance. On the altar, the Nativity of the Virgin, by Sebastiano del Piombo; at the corners, four prophets: Johan by Lorenzetto, Daniel by Bernini, Eliah by Lorenzetto and Habakkuk by Bernini. On the sides, the Tombs of the Chigi family.

Martin Luther, an Augustinian monk, stayed in the convent nextdoor during his visit to Rome at the beginning of the 16th century.

The church stands on the lower slopes of the **PINCIO** gardens, designed by Valadier in 1810. There is a wonderful view from the high terrace: in the distance St. Peter's and the Vatican dominated by the Dome of Michelangelo, the largest one ever built, in the most brilliant sky. People come here to admire the famous Roman sunsets.

We now enter one of the most beautiful parks in the city, **Villa Borghese**. Immediately after the election of Paolo V Borghese as pope, his young nephew Scipione was made cardinal. Among the many titles which he held in that period, Scipione was entrusted with care of the art collection and cultural treasures of the pontifical court. With the help of two able architects, Flaminio Ponzio and Giovanni Van Santen (also known as Vasanzio), Cardinal Scipione created the park and built the **Casino Borghese** (Villa Pinciana), today the site of the **BORGHESE MUSEUM AND GALLERY**.

Scipione was a passionate collector of art and a bold, attentive patron, he sponsored various artists, including Bernini, Caravaggio, Domenichino, Guido Reni and Rubens, and wanted to build the Casino to serve as a cultural landmark where innumerable works of art would be brought together. The villa was also the diplomatic headquarters of the pontifical court, projecting a full sense of the re-risen magnificence of Ancient Rome and setting the example for a new style: the Roman Baroque. Even the surrounding park was once a permanent exhibit in the open-air of statues, fountains and antique sculptures made for Scipione Borghese, including

← *Trinità dei Monti Church and*
  the Boat-shaped Fountain in the foreground.

those used to decorate the welcoming façade of the Casino, with a stairway resembling that of the Campidoglio, designed by Flaminio Ponzio.

Later, between 1770 and 1800, Marcantonio IV Borghese made notable improvements and enlarged the park, adding the Giardino del Lago and building many small buildings. Further additions include Piazza di Siena, the Hippodrome and the zoological gardens.

A few years later, his son Camillo, who had married Pauline Bonaparte, sister of Napoleon, was forced to cede 334 pieces of the magnificent collection to the Louvre. In 1902, because of a heavy financial loss, Prince Paolo Borghese had to sell Villa Borghese with all that it now contains to the Italian government; the park was turned over to the City of Rome, the Casino with its artwork to the Italian State.

Reopened to the public in 1997 (visits by reservation) after many years of restoration, the Galleria Borghese and its many art treasures can again be admired and enjoyed.

On the first floor, the portico features antique reliefs and sculpture. Above are two 16th century reliefs made from designs by Michelangelo: **Prometheus Bound** and **Leda and the Swan**. The grandiosity of the salon which follows leaves the visitor breathless for the richness of the decorations, stuccoes, gold and colors which adorn it.

The fresco on the vault represents the **Apotheosis of Romulus to Jupiter's Olympus**, by the painter Mariano Rossi (1775-1778). On the wall above is a great equestrian monument representing **Marcus Curtius** in the act of throwing himself into the gorge of the Roman Forum, sacrificing himself for the Roman people. Two colossal statues from the 2nd century AD, a **Satyr** and a **Bacchus**, fill the niches. On the floor is a **mosaic with gladiators** which dates to 320 AD.

In the First Room, the visitor's attention is immediately drawn to the neoclassical statue by Canova (1805-1808) of **Pauline Borghese** in the pose of Venus Victrix; on the ceiling the **Judgment of Parides** recalls the subject of the sculpture.

The Second Room takes its name from the sculpture at its center, **Bernini's David** (1623), armed with his sling and ready to strike Goliath. For the statue's face and expression, it seems that Bernini used himself in the act of carving the marble as a source of inspiration.

In the center of the Third Room, Bernini's marble group of **Apollo and Daphne** (1622-1625) represents the nymph Daphne transforming herself into a laurel tree to escape from

Apollo. The theme of metamorphosis is continued in two paintings by Dosso Dossi, **Circe** and **Apollo and Daphne**. The Fourth Room is called the Room of the Emperors for its many porphyry busts of Roman emperors, although the highlight is Bernini's sculpture of **Pluto and Proserpina** (1621), showing the god of the underworld in the act of kidnapping Proserpina, the daughter of Gea (Earth). The Fifth Room is that of the **Hermaphrodite**, a 1st century AD sculpture standing in place of a 2nd century AD Hermaphrodite laying on a mattress added by Bernini, which has been in the Louvre since 1807. In the Sixth Room is another magnificent marble group by Bernini, **Aeneas and Anchises** (1618-1620), which represents Aeneas fleeing from Troy, carrying his father Anchises on his shoulders, with his young son Ascanius. The Seventh Room is known as the Egyptian Room. The Eighth Room, called the room of Silenus or the Faun, is dominated by the **Dancing Faun** (2nd century). This room also holds six of the twelve paintings by Caravaggio that once belonged to the collection of Cardinal Scipione.

On the upper floor is the **Pinacoteca**, made up of twelve rooms, in which we can admire numerous works by painters from the 16th century schools of Florence, Ferrara, Venice and Siena. In addition, there are paintings by artists such as **Raphael**, **Pinturicchio**, **Perugino**, **Scarsellino** and **the Leda**, which is attributed to **Leonardo da Vinci**. In other rooms are 16th century Italian and Florentine Mannerist paintings. A highlight of the museum is the **Gallery of Lanfranco**, decorated by the artist in 1624 with a fresco of the Council of the Gods. In addition, the gallery features pictures from the 19th century, four tondi by **Francesco Albani**, self-portraits, several works by **Guido Reni**, and paintings and small sculptures by **Gian Lorenzo Bernini**.

The Twentieth Room is rich with works by noted artists such as **Antonello da Messina**, **Lorenzo Lotto**, **Giorgione** and **Veronese**. Not to be missed are three marvellous paintings by **Titian**: **Sacred and Profane Love**, **Venus Blindfolding Cupid** and **St. Dominic**.

Piazza del Popolo.

The Olympic Stadium.

7th itinerary
(see map)

From Piazza Venezia to St. Angel Castle

St. Mary Sopra Minerva • The Pantheon
Navona Square • Hadrian's Mausoleum

SANTA MARIA SOPRA MINERVA, the only large Gothic church in Rome, was designed by the Dominican friars that built Santa Maria Novella in Florence (1280-1290) and is a real museum of art and history.

Under the high altar, in a marble sarcophagus lies the Body of **St. Catherine of Siena** (1347-1380). Her greatest glory consists in having persuaded the Pope to return to Rome, after the "Babylonian captivity" of the Church had lasted seventythree years.

In the choir are the tombs of two Popes of the Medici Family. On the left, the **Tomb of Leo X** designed by Baccio Bandinelli (1493-1560), the Florentine sculptor, follower of Michelangelo; the statue is by Raffaello di Montelupo. Leo X (1513-1521), the son of Lorenzo the Magnificent, was a great patron of the arts and deserves a prominent position among the popes: artists and intellectuals soon came to know his benevolence. He raised the Church to a high level, because of his love of all that could extend human knowledge or make life beautiful. This is why he also experienced great bitterness. It was in his reign that Luther started the Reformation. On the right is the **Tomb of Clement VII** (1523-1534).

On the left of the altar stands the famous **statue of Christ** with the cross, sculpted by Michelangelo between 1514 and 1521. Immediately to the left is the monumental slab of Brother **Giovanni da Fiesole** (1387-1455), one of the greatest painters of the Italian 15th century, known as Beato Angelico. Everybody knew of his inimitable religious paintings, in which he was able to blend his total faith which was still medieval, with painting skills of the Renaissance.

The **obelisk of Minerva**, in the square of the same name, stood originally in front of the temple of Isis. It was put here by order of Alexander VII in 1667. Bernini whimsically set the obelisk on the back of an elephant, a work of Ferrata, one of his best pupils.

The **PANTHEON**, a glory of the Eternal City, is the most perfect of all classical monuments in Rome. The inscription on the architrave of the portico "M. Agrippa L. F. Cos tertium fecit" refers to a temple erected by Agrippa in 27 B.C. to the tutelary divinities of the Julia family. For a long time, it was thought that the Pantheon, as it is today, was the original temple of Agrippa. In reality Agrippa's building was destroyed by a great fire in A.D. 80. Recent studies have proved that the present Pantheon is a reconstruction of the time of Hadrian. Other alterations were made at the time of Septimius Severus and of Caracalla. On the 6th March 609, Boniface IV, with the permission of Emperor Phocas, changed the pagan temple into a Christian church dedicating it to St. Mary of the Martyrs. It is to this fact we owe the preservation of the Pantheon. The bodies of many martyrs were removed from the Catacombs to be buried here. As a sanctuary, in virtue of the Lateran Pact, it acquired the status of palatine basilica or, in other words, of the national church of all Italians.

The **portico** is supported by 16 monolithic granite columns; in the tympanum there was a bas-relief in bronze representing the battle of gods and giants. The ceiling of the portico was covered with bronze. This precious material, weighing about 450.000 lbs, was removed by order of Urban VIII (1623-1644) and used by Bernini for the high altar at St. Peter's and other works. It was precisely the removal of the bronze from the ceiling, which inspired Pasquino, the famous "talking statue", to make the "pasquinate" or quip: "What the barbarians did not do, the Barberini did"! In the two niches, statues of Augustus and Agrippa once stood. The **bronze doors** are original.

The **interior** measures 43,40 meters in diameter, and the same in height. Light and air still enter through the opening at the top (a circle of 8 m. 92 cms in diameter, which still retains part of the original bronze-covered rim). Heaven itself seems to pour into this temple left open so that prayers could freely ascend. All this gives an impression of unequalled solemnity: its simple regularity, the beauty of its proportions and the splendid materials used, combine to make the interior sublime. The solemn **dome** is in fact a cap, whose thickness gradually dimishes from the bottom to the top. All around are seven niches. In the centre stood the statue of Jove Ultor who pun-

The Pantheon.

*Inside
of the Pantheon.*

ished the assassins of Caesar; in the others were statues of the chief divinities. Other gods and heroes were in the intermediary spaces. Only the splendid columns of antique yellow marble remain to give us an idea of its primitive splendour.

Sovereigns and artists have their tombs in the Pantheon. In the first chapel to the left repose the **remains of Perin del Vaga** (1500-1547), considered second only to Giulio Romano among Raphael's pupils.

Next is the **tomb of Baldassarre Peruzzi** (1481-1536), a great painter and architect.

In the second chapel are the **tombs of King Umberto I** and **Queen Margherita** (1851-1926).

Between the second and third chapels the tomb that contains the earthly remains of Raphael, one of the most popular artists in the world, whose epigraph says: "Living, great Nature feared he might outlive her works; and dying, fears herself to die". The **Statue of Madonna** is the work of his pupil Lorenzetto.

Close by is the **tomb of Maria Bibbiena**, his promised wife, who died three months before him. Above is the **tomb of Annibale Caracci** (1560-1609).

In the third chapel we see the **Cenotaph of Cardinal Consalvi** (1755-1824) an exquisite work by Thorwaldsen (1820-1878). In the sixth chapel, is the **tomb of Victor Emanuel II** (1820-1878). At the altar of the seventh chapel, a fresco of the **Annunciation**, by Melozzo da Forli.

A stone's throw away in the Via della Scrofa, is the Church of **St. Louis of the French**, the national church of the French in Rome. The late Renaissance facade is by Giacomo della Porta. Inside, there are superb frescoes by Domenichino in the "Chapel of S. Cecilia", and on the altar is a copy by Guido Reni of **St. Cecilia** by Raphael, whose original is in Bologna. Without a doubt, this church's gems are the wonderful Caravaggio paintings of the **life of Saint Matthew** which were hung here in the St. Matthew chapel in 1600.

The **PIAZZA NAVONA**, or "Circo Agonale", occupies the place of the Stadium of Domitian, that could hold 30.000 spectators. Here are three magnificent fountains. The one in the centre, "an Aesop's fable fashioned in marble" is the **Fountain of the Four Rivers** by Bernini, who made it as a base for the Egyptian obelisk brought here from the Circus of Maxentius.

The Pantheon and Piazza Navona in the days of Imperial Rome.

The **Church of Sant'Agnese in Agone**, is built on the spot where, according to tradition, the virgin, denuded before her martyrdom, was mantled in her hair, which had grown miraculously to cover her. It is a magnificent Baroque building designed by G. Rainaldi and Borromini. Beneath it are some remains of the original church and of the Circus of Domitian. In the vicinity is the **Church of St. Mary of Peace**, where over the arch of the first chapel to the right we see the celebrated group of the **Sibyls** by Raphael. The fine portico of the façade is by Pietro da Cortona.

The cloister is adjacent to the church. It was made by Bramante, his first work after he arrived in Rome (1500-1504), and after the significant experience he had gained in Lombardy. Actually, thanks to its geometrical clarity merging with the subtle play of proportions which best expresses the Renaissance spirit, Bramante regained the trust of the Papal court and especially of Julius II. So the artist was put in charge of the main architectural works of the splendid Rome of the Renaissance. As we shall see, he provided the decisive impulse for the building of the new basilica of St. Peter in the Vatican, and he also left his mark on other works which were smaller in size but no less important.

Another portion of the collection of the Museo Nazionale Romano is on display in **PALAZZO ALTEMPS**, on Via Sant'Apollinare. The palace, begun before 1477 by Girolamo Riario, was finished by Cardinal Marco Sittico Altemps and his heirs around 1570. In the sixteenth century, Cardinal Altemps gathered a large collection of antique sculpture and an extremely rich library, which were subsequently broken up. The palace, restored by the Superintendent of Archaeology of Rome, is today home to the **Ludovisi Boncompagni Collection**, the **Egyptian Collection** of the Museo Nazionale Romano, the **Mattei Collection**, some pieces from other collections, and just sixteen sculptures that remain from the Altemps collection. The Ludovisi Boncompagni Collection was begun by Cardinal Ludovico Ludovisi between 1621 and 1623 in a villa on the Quirinal Hill, and was enriched over the years, especially by the new owner of the Villa Gregorio Boncompagni, by the 19th century it contained 339 sculptures. Many works were brought together through state acquisitions in 1901.

There are many works of great interest on the ground floor of the palazzo. The courtyard is without doubt the most remark-

Piazza Navona .

St. Angel's Castle and Bridge.

A magnificent view of Piazza Navona, by night.

able, having been worked on by Antonio Sangallo the Elder, Baldassarre Peruzzi and Martino Longhi. Built at the same time as the courtyard, the southern portico is decorated with family crests of the Orsini and Altemps. Like the northern portico, it holds sculptures from the Mattei collection of the Villa Celimontana. The atrium is named after Antonino Pius for the nude statue of an emperor which it hosts. Also on the first floor are ten display rooms rich with statues, sarcophagi, portraits, herms and ornamental vases. Among them are the beautiful statues of **Apollo Citaredo**, the **Athena** (with head and limbs restored by Algardi), and the **Athena Parthenos** from the Ludovisi Collection. Also notable is the colossal group of **Dionysius**, the **Satyr and the panther**, a Roman copy of a Greek original.

A monumental stairway leads to the first floor, which contains the **Southern Loggia** and the **Painted Loggia**; many display rooms; the private rooms of the Cardinal, with several busts; and those of the **Duchessa Isabella Lante Altemps**, with the **Bathing Aphrodite** by Diodalsas, **Eros and Psyche**, a composition of ancient works created by Algardi. In the Room of the Fireplace is **Galata Killing himsel**, **with his wife**, to which belonged the Dying Galata which hangs today in the Capitoline Museums.

CASTEL SANT'ANGELO. The Queen of Halicarnassus, wife of King Mausolus, erected for her husband a magnificent tomb, one of the wonders of the world. It was called Mausoleum, and this name has been used ever since for tombs of large dimensions. **The Mausoleum of Hadrian** surpassed in dimensions and magnificence every other tomb. We get no idea of it from what remains. It would require too great an effort of imagination to re-evoke all its splendour. Procopius, the Byzantine historian of the 6th century, left us a description of it in his time. The Mausoleum had square foundations above which rose a big tower adorned with doric columns, statues and spaces for epitaphs of the dead. On the top was a colossal group representing Hadrian in a chariot drawn by four horses. All the enormously thick walls were faced with Parian marble. It was, after the Colosseum, the most splendid example of Roman architecture.

At the death of the Emperor, the Mausoleum was not yet finished; his successor Antoninus Pius brought his remains to Rome. His successors and princes of imperial families were buried here until Caracalla. The history of Hadrian's

Mausoleum follows the history of Rome and both saw the struggles and treachery of the Middle Ages, the splendour of the Papal Court in the Renaissance, the horrors of the Sack of Rome in 1527, the furious bombardments during many sieges, and inoffensive fireworks of festivities.

Under Aurelian (275) but more probably under Honorius (403) it was strongly fortified and incorporated in the city walls in order to form a real bastion, in defense of the banks of the Tiber. This strategic function came into evidence in the first invasion of the barbarians led by Alaric in 410. It was probably transformed into a castle in the 10th century, when it fell into the hands of Alberich and his mother, Marozia, powerful figures in Rome at the time, whose alternating fortunes reflect the city's contemporary history. It then passed to the Crescenzis and in 1277 it was occupied by Nicholas III who connected it to the Vatican by the famous corridor, a safety passage which runs along the top of the encircling wall of the Vatican. Henceforth, it remained under the control of the Popes who used it as a fortress, to impress, but also as a prison and a place for torture.

The Castle is divided into five floors (when visiting it, follow the numbers marked in the rooms for this purpose). **Floor I** (Grond floor) from which starts the famous winding ramp about 400 feet long, a stupendous Roman costruction.

After the ramp, continuing to climb to the left by the "cordonata" (stone-ribbed gradient) of Alexander VI we reach the third floor in the Court of the Angel. **Floor II** (or floor of the prisons) with horrible cells, called "historical" prisons, and store-rooms for wheat and oil. One descends from the upper floor (Court of Alexander VI). **Floor III** (or military floor) with two big courtyards. The first is the Courtyard of the Angel (or the Court of the Cannon Balls) in the middle of which there stands the marble Angel by Giacomo della Porta, which stood at the top of the Castle until 1752. There are also several heaps of stone balls, projectiles of bygone times. In the first room of Clement VIII are models in clay reproducing the Castle in various periods.

The other court is the Court of Alexander VI with a fine 16th century marble well. A tiny staircase leads to an interesting small bath-room of Clement VII decorated with frescoes by Giulio Romano. In the rooms facing the two courts military equipment is exhibited of various periods. **Floor IV** (or papal floor), with the loggia of Julius II, by Bramante, in the principal part of the castle and the papal apartment, consisting of magnificent rooms with frescoes by Giulio Romano, Perin del Vaga and other painters of Raphael's school, the Sala del Tesoro and Cagliostro's Room, the prison cell of the famous alchemist of the 18th century. **Floor V** (top floor) with a big terrace, dominated by an Archangel in bronze by Wersschaffelt, from which we have a fine panorama of the city.

8th itinerary
(see map)

The Appian Way

The Baths of Caracalla · Quo Vadis · The Catacombs
The Tomb of Cecilia Metella

No other road is so well known in the world as the **Via Appia**. Proudly called the "Regina Viarum", it was begun by Appius Claudius in 312 B.C. Bordering it for many miles, were sepulchres and tomb-stones of twenty generations. Only patrician families could have tombs here. Here were the tombs of the Scipios, Furii, Manili, Sestili.
The first part of the Appian Way is called Via Porta San Sebastiano. At the beginning, the famous **Baths of Caracalla** or Antoninian Baths, begun by Septimius Severus in 206 and inaugurated in 217 by Caracalla, although finished by his successors Heliogabal and Alexander Severus. Sixteen hundred persons could bathe here at the same time. So vast were the baths that to the eyes of Ammianus Marcellinus they seemed like provinces. There were rooms for cold, hot and warm baths, splendid ceilings, porticoes, pillared halls, gymnasiums, where the rarest marbles, the most colossal columns, the finest statues were admired by the people; even the baths were of basalt, granite, alabaster.
Still today, the size and the majesty of the ruins of this great complex are impressive.
On the Via di Porta S. Sebastiano, close to the junction with the Via di Porta Latina and the Church of St. Cesario, is **Bessarion's Lodge**, called after the celebrated humanist, Cardinal Bessarion who was of Byzantine origin and contributed to spreading the cult of classical antiquity in Renaissance Rome.
The Cardinal restored this house, that was built at the beginning of the 14th century, and offered hospitality to the most illustrious humanists of Italy and Greece: Flavio Biondo, Filelfo, Poggio, Campano, Platina, and others who gathered around the Greek cardinal "in those meetings in which they spoke of art, science, and especially of Platonic philosophy". After the death of the Cardinal (1472) the Lodge was abandoned, and it was reduced to the status

Via Appia Antica.

of a small country inn. In 1930, properly restored, this precious architectural treasure was restored to its ancient grace. Many years after its discovery, when most pieces of archeological value had unfortunately already been removed, the **Sepulchre of the Scipios**, a severe Roman monument, was enclosed within a large park between 1926 and 1929. The monument is more complicated than its name implies. A 4th century **Roman house** and **Christian catacombs** may also be visited within this archeological park, as well as the famous family's sepulchre. By opening up a well which is 40 feet deep, nine tenths of the sepulchre have been made visible.

Before passing the Porta Appia or Porta San Sebastiano, we see the so-called **Arch of Drusus**.

The **Porta San Sebastiano** (former Porta Appia) is in the Aurelian Wall, begun by Aurelius in 272, finished by Probus in 279. It is well preserved.

At this point, the most famous part of the Appian Way begins. It is marked by landmarks of specific importance, such as the **Quo Vadis** Chapel, where, according to a holy legend, Peter had a vision of Christ.

Nero persecuted the Christians to calm the fury of the people against him for the burning of Rome. St. Peter was asked by the Christians to leave Rome for a while until the persecution was over. He consented but not far from Porta Appia, he met a traveller going towards Rome. Peter recognized him and asked: "Domine, quo vadis?" ("Lord, where are you going?"). And Jesus answered, "I am going to Rome to be crucified for the second time!" The vision vanished, but the imprint of the divine feet remains on the stone in the road. This was the legend recorded by Origen. (254).

Facing the Quo Vadis Chapel, stands the circular ruin of **the tomb of Priscilla** the beloved wife of Abascanzius, a freed slave and a favourite of Domitian, who died young. Statius, (45-96) perhaps the best poet of the time, included in his "Sylvae", a short poem in her honour.

As well as vestiges of classical Rome, the Appian Way offers us the most suggestive evidence of early Christianity. Indeed, some of the most famous Roman **Catacombs** (as these ancient subterranean Christian cemeteries have been incorrectly known since the 19th century), extend in all directions beneath it. In fact, the areas destined by the Christians for burial places, used to be called "coemeteria", (resting place) while the term "catacomba" originally served to indicate the specific locality beneath the actual Basilica of St. Sebastian, where the land was characterized by a pronounced subsidence.

The Catacombs of St. Callixtus, St. Sebastian and Domitilla, are the most frequently visited and venerated. Guided tours are compulsory, so only a brief explanation is necessary.

The **Catacombs of St. Callixtus** show us the first Christian cemetery of the Christian Community in Rome, to administer which Pope Zephyrinus (199-217) chose the deacon Callixtus, who was later Pope from 217 to 222. The Salesians are now their custodians.

The **Catacombs of St. Sebastian** (over which since the 4th century is a magnificent basilica in honour of the Apostles Peter and Paul), received the precious relic of the martyr of the same name.

The excavations begun in 1915 and continuing today, have brought to light a particularly important series of buildings, dedicated to the memory of the two Apostles up to the third century. It may justly be said that they form the most important monument of underground Christian Rome. The Franciscans are the custodians of these Catacombs.

The **Catacombs of Domitilla**, are called by the name of the Christian lady to whom this land belonged. She was a member of the imperial family of the Flavians. These are possibly the most extensive catacombs in Rome. In this area, stands the 4th century **Basilica of St. Nereo and St. Achilles**, which was discovered in 1874 and subsequently restored.

Between the Via Ardeatina and the Via delle Sette Chiese, at a short distance from the Catacombs of St. Sebastian, there is another place of martyrdom and sacrifice: the **Fosse Ardeatine** (Ardeatine Graves).

Just as the first Christians were innocent victims because of their heroic faith, so in this almost abandoned neighbourhood, at dawn on March 24, 1944, 335 Italians, mainly Jews, were the victims of the inhuman nazi fury. Today, a grave and simple crypt preserves the same number of remains in sarcophagi, lined up in their death as in their martyrdom.

The **Temple of Romulus** was erected by Maxentius, his father, in the 4th century A.D. This Emperor also built the splendid Circus which bears his name. Unearthed in 1825, it is a magnificent complex: on the ample, harmonious rolling hills of the Roman countryside, as well as the ruins of the circus with its typical cylindrical towers, are those of a **villa**, also attributed to Maxentius (4th century A.D.).

The **Tomb of Cecilia Metella** stands solemnly on the brow of a hill on the Appian way. Cecilia was the wife of Crassus, a member, with Caesar and Pompey, of the First Triumvirate which ended the Roman Republic, paving the way for the Empire (1st century B.C.). On her tomb, which was turned into a fortress in the middle ages, the original commemorative slab still remains. From here to the IVth mile, the Appian Way remains as it has been since it was redesigned in the mid-19th century as a romantic road, littered with ancient sepulchres which have mostly been reconstructed.

The whole road, according to the original urban plan of 1931, was intended to be surrounded by a vast protected area, from St. Sebastian's Gate to the limits of the Municipality of Rome and beyond. This was to be the famous "Archeological Park of the Appian Way" which exists on maps more convincingly than in reality, and was supposed to link up with the "Archeological Park of the Imperial Forums" in the heart of Rome, according to a project which has yet to be implemented.

Catacombs of St. Sebastian.

Catacombs of St. Callixtus.

Catacombs of Domitilla.

9th itinerary
(see map)

The Vatican City

St. Peter's Basilica • The Vatican Museums
The Sistine Chapel

The **Vatican** has been the residence of the popes since 1377, only six centuries. Before the pontifical court was transferred to Avignon, (1309-1377), the headquarters of the papacy were at the Lateran. From that time, it can be said that there has not been a pope who has failed to contribute to its grandeur and its dignity, to make this holy hill an increasingly worthy seat for the Supreme Head of the Catholic Church. An uninterrupted succession of 264 men have sat on Peter's throne, many of whom were martyrs and saints.
Since February 11, 1929, the Vatican has consisted of an independent State called **Vatican City**, by virtue of the Lateran Treaties which resolved the Roman Issue between the Italian State and the Church.
In the Roman era, the Vatican hill was the site of the Circus Neronianus where under Nero, St. Peter the Apostle was crucified. His body was buried nearby and more than two hundred and fifty years later Constantine built a magnificent basilica on this spot, destined to become one of the marvels of the world. During the seventy-three years that the Popes were in Avignon, the basilica was so neglected that it was almost impossible to restore it. Nicholas V decided to reconstruct it giving the project to Rossellino. At the death of the Pope, the work was suspended.
It was Julius II (1503-1513) who began the construction of the new basilica. To design it, he commissioned Bramante who was to play the main role in this ambitious architectural enterprise, which took 176 years of work to complete. During all these years, various projects succeeded one another (Raphael, Sangallo, etc.), until Michelangelo, almost seventy years old, began to build the dome.
After his death the work went on according to his plans, based on the Greek cross as had been intended by Bramante. However, in Paul V's time, Maderno finally adopted the design based on the shape of a Latin cross.

MAP OF ST. PETER'S

1 Atrium
2 Portal of the Dead
3 Central Portal (Filarete)
4 Holy Door
5 Nave
6 Chapel of the Pietà
7 Monument to Leo XII
8 Monument to Christina of Sweden
9 Monument to Pius XI
10 Chapel of St. Sebastian
11 Monument to Pius XI
12 Monument to Innocent XII
13 Monument to the Countess Mathilde
14 Chapel of the Blessed Sacrament
15 Monument to Gregory XIII
16 Monument to Gregory XIV
17 Monument to Gregory XVI
18 Gegorian Chapel
19 Altar of Our Lady of Succour
20 Altar of St. Jerome
21 Altar of St. Basil
22 Monument to Benedict XIV
23 Right transept
24 Altar of St. Wenceslas
25 Altar of Sts. Processus and Martinian
26 Altar of St.Erasmus
27 Altar of the Incense-boat
28 Monument to Clement XIII
29 Altar of the Archangel Michael
30 Altar of St. Petronilla
31 Altar of St. Peter and the Resuscitation of Tabitha
32 Monument to Clement X
33 Nave of the Throne
34 Monument to Urban VIII
35 St Peter's Throne
36 Monument to Paul III
37 Monument to Alexander VIII
38 Altar of St. Peter and the Healing of the Cripple
39 Chapel of the Column
40 Altar of St. Leo the Great
41 Altar of the Column
42 Monument to Alexander VII
43 Altar of the Sacred Heart
44 Left Transept
45 Altar of St. Thomas
46 Altar of St. Joseph
47 Altar of the Crucifiixion of St. Peter
48 Statue of St. Veronica
49 Statue of St. Helena
50 Statue of St. Longinus
51 Statue of St. Peter
52 Confession and Papal Altar
53 Statue of St. Andrew (entrance to Grottoes)
54 A ltar of the Falsehood
55 Monument to Pius VIII (door to Sacristy and treasury)
56 Clementine Chapel
57 Altar of St. Gregory
58 Monument to Pius VII
59 Altar of the transfiguartion
60 Monument to Leo XI
61 Monument to Innocent XI
62 Chapel of the Choir
63 Altar of the Immaculate Conception
64 Monument to Pius X
65 Monument to Innocent VIII
66 Monument to John XXIII
67 Chapel of the Presentation of the Virgin
68 Monument to Benedict XV
69 Monument to Maria Clementina Sobiesky (entrance to Dome)
70 Stuart Monument
71 Baptistery

St. Peter's Square is by far largest in Rome.

The Basilica of St. Peter - Inside.

The Vatican - Aerial view.

Let us now admire St. Peter's square, in front of the greatest church of Christianity: **ST. PETER'S IN THE VATICAN**. The square is unique. It is dominated by the immense suggestive **dome**, by Michelangelo. It is a harmonious poem of immensity. The dome rises gigantic against the background of the sky and its silver-blue colour merges with the same tint of the heavenly dome of which it seems the architectural synthesis. When Michelangelo's immortal genius conceived it, he must have perceived this sense of the absolute and infinite that would impress the soul of whoever saw it. The **colonnade** is the finest work of Bernini and forms a superb entry to St. Peter's and the Vatican.

The two large wings opening like half circles seem like the two outstretched arms of the temple receiving all mankind in one universal embrace. Nothing more harmonious can be imagined.

The erection of the **obelisk** roused great wonder and enthusiasm in the people. After conferring with many architects Sixtus V, decided to assign this work to Domenico Fontana. It was begun on the 3rd of April 1586 and the enormous monolith was raised on September 10th, in the presence of a great crowd, with the aid of nine hundred men.

The **two fountains**, the one on the right, designed by Maderno in 1613, and the one on the left, in 1677 by Carlo Fontana, harmonize perfectly with the vast square.

In very large letters, right across the broad **facade** of the Basilica, the work of Maderno (1607-1614), are written the name and title of Paul V Borghese, who commissioned it. The **Loggia of the Benedictions**, above the central entrance, is used to proclaim the election of every new Pope and it is from here that he delivers his first blessing "Urbi et orbi" (to the city and the world).

Inside the **portico**, above the main entrance, is the famous **Navicella** (little ship), designed by Giotto during the first Jubilee year, and which has undergone a lot of restoration. Five doors open on to the portico, corresponding to the Basilica's five aisles.

The first door on the left is the **Door of Death** by Manzù, which shows the death of Jesus and that of the Madonna, the death of Pope John XXIII and death in space (1952-1964). The **bronze door**, designed by Filarete, an imitation of the one by Ghiberti at Florence, was also in the old basilica. The **Porta Santa** (Holy Door) is opened only every twenty-five years. On these occasions on Christmas Eve, the Pope, following a special rite, goes in solemn procession to this door, and after a triple genuflection and three strokes of a hammer, the wall is removed and the Pope enters first. At the end of the Jubilee year the door is shut with special solemnities. The modern reliefs which decorate it, are by Vico Consorti.

Another two contemporary doors complete the portico, the **Door of Good** and **Evil** by Minguzzi and the **Door of the Sacraments**, by Crocetti.

And now let us enter the church, which is the impressive sanctuary of Christ built over the tomb of his first Vicar. The main altar, beneath Michelangelo's dome, stands over the **tomb of St. Peter**, definitively identified after the excavations carried out in the '50s and '60s, which will be mentioned in our description of the Sacred Grottoes. Before us, burning day and night, flicker ninety-five lamps.

Under the *Papal Altar*, reserved to the Pontiff, there is the **Confession** in which two semicircular flights of steps go down toward the level of the old Consantine Basilica arisen next to the Tomb of the Apostle and Confessor of his faith (that's exactly the term of Confession).

Over the altar, the famous **canopy** of Bernini, upheld by four spiral columns, made with bronze taken from the Pantheon. But the glorification of the tomb of the humble fisherman of Galilee is the majestic **dome** rising up to the sky, the multiple choirs of angels and blessed souls around the throne of the Most High in a glory of light, harmony and immensity.

In the niches of the colossal pillars are four statues: St. Andrew, by Duquesnoy; St. Veronica, by Mochi; St. Helena, by Bolgi; St. Longinus, by Bernini.

On the right of the pillar of St. Longinus, seated on a throne, is the celebrated **bronze statue of St. Peter**. Now let us start the tour of the basilica.

In the first chapel of the right aisle above the altar, we admire the **Pietà**, one of the most beautiful works of young Michelangelo. The name of the young artist is chiselled on the sash that goes over the Madonna's shoulder. On the knees of the immortally young Virgin lies the body of Christ who seems asleep. The Olympian severity of their beautiful figures is surrounded by a veil of sadness.

The **monument of Christine of Sweden**, on the first pillar, is by Carlo Fontana; the bas-relief by Théodon represents the ceremony at Innsbruck when Christine

Carlo Fontana's Fountain in St. Peter's Square.

Roman buggy in St. Peter's Square.

The majestic Dome of St. Peter's, by Michelangelo,

became Catholic, changing her name to Alexandra.
The **monument to Countess Mathilda of Canossa**, on the second pillar, is all of white marble and was erected in 1635 by Bernini who also modelled the beautiful statue of the Countess; the bas-relief, the work of Stefano Speranza, represents the humiliation which the Emperor Henry IV suffered at Canossa, at the hands of Pope Gregory VII (1077).
In the "Chapel of the Blessed Sacrament", above the altar, is Bernini's **Tabernacle**, which recalls the architecture of the "Tempietto" by Bramante, in San Pietro in Montorio.
We pass by on the right of the fine **monument to Gregory XIII** (1572-85) by Rusconi.
On the left we pass into the "Gregorian Chapel", the **monument to Pope Gregory XVI** is the work of the sculptor Amici. Gregory XVI (1832-1846) was a patron of fine arts. He founded three museums: the Etruscan, the Egytian and the Museum of Ancient sculpture formerly at the Lateran, but which today is integrated with the other two among the numerous collections in the Vatican Museums.
In the aisle after the transept, on the right is the **monument to Clement XIII** (1758-1769), one of Canova's best works. He spent more than six years preparing the design, the models, and actually making it.
In the Tribune, four Doctors of the Church support the **Throne of St. Peter**, a talented and lively work by Bernini, which encloses the ancient wooden seat of the first Basilica; it was identified, thanks to recent research, as the throne of Constantine. Above is a luminous round stained-glass window, portraying the Holy Spirit in the form of a dove, surrounded by a dynamic vortex of clouds and angels.
To the right, is the **monument to Urban VIII**, celebrated work of the same artist. During the pontificate of this Pope, St. Peter's was finished after many years (1626). To the left, the **monument to Paul III** (1534-49) a real secular prince of the Renaissance, by Guglielmo della Porta, is perhaps the finest work of this artist in St. Peter's.
Let us now enter the **Chapel of the Column**, behind St. Veronica's pillar. Above the **altar of St. Leo Magnu**s, we admire one of the largest bas-reliefs in the world, by Algardi: the two principal figures are about ten feet high. It represents one of the principal events of our civilisation: the **Meeting of Leo I with Attila** (452), during which the defenceless Pope succeeded, by his prestige alone, in halting the invasion of the terrible King of the Huns.

Beyond the transept, on the opposite side, is the **Clementine Chapel**. Under the altar is the **Body of St. Gregorius Magnus**, the last of the four Doctors of the Latin Church. To the left of the altar rises the **monument to Pius VII** (1800-23) by the Danish sculptor A. Thorvaldsen.

The **Chapel of the Choir** is used for daily choral services. In the second pillar is the **monument to Innocent VIII**, by Pollaiolo. Among the glories of his pontificate, the inscription recalls the discovery of a New World. The Pope, a Genoese, died on the 26th of July 1492; two months later, another Genoese discovered America.

Opposite we admire the **monument to St. Pius X**, (1903-14) who died a few months after the outbreak of World War I. It is an admirable work by the sculptor Astorri and the architect Di Fausto.

In the **Chapel of the Presentation**, on the left, rises one of the last monuments erected in St. Peter's, **the monument to Benedict XV**, the Pope of Peace; it is noted for the rich marbles and fine sculpture, by Canonica.

Close by, is the door by which we ascend to the Dome. Over the door the **monument to Maria Clementina Sobiesky**, wife of James Stuart, the Old Pretender. Opposite, in the first pillar, the **monument to the last Stuart**, exquisite work by Canova (1817-19). The **baptismal font** ends the left aisle.

This huge building reveals itself as a succession of majestic halls each of which looks almost like a large cathedral. The figures are eloquent.

The length of the interior of the Basilica, as revealed by a writing traced on the floor near the bronze gate, is 691 feet. (The outside length including the porch is 694 feet). There follow more writings indicating the length of the largest churches in the world. The vault is 144 feet high. An arcade of the central nave is 75 feet (nearly equal to the obelisk of the square). The dome, inside, is 390 feet high; the lantern is over 55 feet high. Its diameter is 137 feet nearly equal to that of the Pantheon (142), which however, it less high. The perimeter of each of the four pillars supporting the dome, is 232 feet. The statues in the respective niches are over 16 feet tall. The pen of the Evangelist St. Mark, in the medallion above the pillar of St. Helena, is 5 ft. high! The canopy is 95 ft., over 13 ft. higher than the obelisk.

And if the Church is observed from above (for instance from the interior rail of the dome), one feels really giddy.

The Chair of St. Peter in its masterful setting by Bernini.

Inside of the Dome and Canopy of St. Peter's.

THE SACRED GROTTOES

The subsoil of the present Basilica, which corresponds approximately to the level of the original building dating from the period of Constantine is of particular interest. It is reached from inside the Basilica, to be precise, by a stairway within one of the great pillars which support the dome, which opens out into a semi-circular gallery known as the **New Grottoes.** In fact, this is the most ancient part, but it was opened later, hence its name.

Excavations under the Confession have led to the basic discovery that Pope Paul VI announced on June 26, 1968: "The relics of Peter have been identified in a way which we may consider convincing".

Four oratories open on to the gallery, and several chapels, in one of which is the **Tomb of Pope Pius XII**. From this hall the vast space of the **Old Grottoes** is reached, which extend under the central nave of the upper Basilica, made by Antonio da Sangallo to act as a dampcourse to protect the flooring of the new building. In the fascinating shadows of the three aisles with low vaulted ceilings, and the succession of two rhythmic rows of impressive pillars, the funeral monuments of about twenty popes, an emperor, a king, two queens, numerous cardinals and bishops follow, as well as precious works of art, all records of the old basilica.

THE WAY UP TO THE DOME

The entrance is on the right of the portico. The first part of the climb until one reaches the broad terrace which covers the central nave, can be made in a lift or on foot, up a spiral staircase. The view from the balustrade is fascinating: the Bernini complex in the foreground, then a little further the shining meanders of the Tiber and the city in the distance, make a very harmonious scene. Turning towards the Dome, we are suddenly struck by the restrained tension of the sculpted ribs which run up it to the lantern.

Within, we face a gallery which runs round the drum, 53 m. from the floor of the Basilica. The view from high up is impressive: Bernini's altar canopy, as tall as a palace, looks like a small-scale model from here. In the last part of the ascent, we squeeze between the two superimposed spherical vaults, which are more and more curved as we near the top. Having reached the top of the *lantern*, we can go out to admire the unforgettable view of the city from the circular panoramic balcony.

THE TREASURY

In the Basilica once again, going up the left aisle to the Monument to Pius VIII, under which is the entrance to the Sacristy, one reaches the Museum of Historical Art of St. Peter's, or the Treasury (see map St. Peter's no. 55). Right from the age of Costantine (4th century) the Basilica of St. Peter received outstanding donations many of which came through the Emperor himself. The generosity of the donators was such that in the following centuries, the Treasury was assiduously replenished in spite of the frequency with which it was disastrously plundered, especially on the occasion of the various Jubilees which have taken place since 1300.

Room I - There are a *red cope* with *tiara* decorated with stones (XVIII century) destined to cover the venerated Saint Peter's statue of bronze; the so-called *Chalice Stuart*, itself belonging to the XVIII century, in gold and silver with 130 mounted brilliants. *Room II* - There are exposed some of the most precious works, among which the *Vatican Cross* covered with silver leather and precious stones, containing fragments of the real Cross; the *Dalmatix*, erroneously called of Charlemagne; numerous precious *shrines*. *Room III* is dominated by the *bronze monument to Sixtus IV* (1471-84), a masterpiece by Antonio del Pollaiolo. In *Room IV* is the 14th-century *frame of Veronica* which used to hold the precious relic pressed between two sheets of glass. In *Room V* the visitor can see *copper spheres* used as handwarmers in the chilly sacristies, as well as a collection of *precious chalices* and *reliquaries*. In *Room VI*, a vast collection of *candelabra* is exhibited. The small room that forms the corridor contains large sacred codices. *Room VII* contains a model of one of the *worshipping angels*, made in clay and cast in bronze by Bernini for the Chapel of the Sacrament. *Room VIII* displays a collection of vestments, sacred objects and votive jewels donated to the pontiffs by the faithful from all over the world. *Room IX* contains the *sarcophagus of Junius Bassus* (4th century).

Panoramic view from the Dome of St. Peter's.

Tomb of St. Peter.

Michelangelo's Pietà.

THE VATICAN MUSEUMS

The Vatican Palaces are really a cluster of buildings whose construction began in the Middle Ages and continued under the auspices of numerous popes.

The entrance to the museums is in the northern part of the external section of the Vatican walls. The portal on the Viale Vaticano, 10 meters high, is impressive. It is carved into the massive wall which marks the boundaries of Vatican City State and at the same time, props up the hill. The entrance is surmounted by two large statues of Michelangelo and Raphael which support the coat of arms of Pius XI, during whose pontificate it was built. The doors open into a broad atrium, which leads to the *spiral ramp*, built in 1932 by Giuseppe Momo who struggled to overcome enormous technical difficulties in order to link the entrance level with that of the museums. It has a double flight of steps, for those going up and for those going down. The *bronze balustrade* adorned with classical festoons in relief was made by the sculptor Antonio Maraini. At the top of the ramp is a *circular balcony* where the ticket office is located.

CHIARAMONTI MUSEUM

Access to this museum, either directly or through the Egyptian Museum, is from the beautiful *courtyard of the Pine cone* one of the three sections of the enormous courtyard of the Belvedere designed by Bramante.

The Chiaramonti Museum is called after Pius VII (1800-1823) of the Chiaramonti family; eager to continue the work of his predecessors Clement XIV and Pius VI, he arranged for a large part of the Vatican collections to be housed here. He therefore had Antonio Canova design a long corridor flanking the cortile della Pigna, to contain about 800 sculptures. In addition to this great corridor, called the *Chiaramonti Gallery*, and the adjacent *Lapidary Gallery*, reserved for the use of scholars, the *New Wing* which transversely links these galleries with the parallel Vatican Library is also part of this museum.

The **Braccio nuovo** is a gallery 70 meters long, bordered by numerous niches and widening into an apse in the center where an allegorical representation of the Nile has been placed, a copy of an Alexandrian original from the 1st to the 2nd centuries BC, discovered in 1513 near the Campo Marzio in the heart of Rome.

Among the other valuable statues in this section, we mention the most interesting of the Chiaramonti Museum, the *Augustus of Prima Porta*, named after the Roman neighborhood where it was found. The emperor is shown here in an attitude of regal domination, wearing armor finely decorated in relief. The whole figure exudes a sense of masterful resolution. We also point out the figure of an *Amazon*, a copy of an original by Polycletus, the great Greek sculptor of the 5th century BC who was a contemporary of Phidias. Another important copy is that of the *Doryphorus* (spear-bearer) also by Polycletus, who established the "Kanon", that is, the ideal principles for perfect human proportions.

PIO-CLEMENTINE MUSEUM

The Pio-Clementine Museum owes its name to Clement XIV (1769-1775) and his successor, Pius VI (1775-1799) who was responsible for its final arrangement. It consists of twelve rooms, containing mainly Roman sculptures including numerous copies of Greek originals. Access to the museum today is through the former entrance made by Clement XIV, on the opposite side to the entrance Pius VI had built later. After passing the entrance arch with the inscription "Museum Clementinum", immediately on the left the visitor can admire the famous *sarcophagus of Lucius Cornelius Scipio the Bearded* (consul in 298 BC). Crossing a circular vestibule adorned with a precious funerary altar, the visitor reaches the **Cabinet of the Apoxyomenos** on the right, called after the famous *Apoxyomenos*, the athlete shown using a special instrument to scrape away the oil and sand with which he had covered himself. The statue is the only copy in existence of the Greek original by Lysippus (artist of the 4th century BC). The visitor then immediately finds himself in the **Octagonal Belvedere Courtyard**, not to be confused with the large Belvedere Courtyard that lies between the Library and the Lapidary Gallery. It was only in 1775 that it was given the octagonal form which distinguishes it today, with the addition of the portico by Michelangelo Simonetti, the architect responsible for organizing this museum. Subsequently, beneath the portico surrounding the courtyard, Canova closed off four small areas known as gabinetti "cabinets" which house some of the Vatican Museums best known statues. These are: the **Cabinet of the Belvedere Apollo**, with a marble copy of the bronze 4th-century BC Apollo that came to light at the end of the 15th century and was set here by Julius II together with several other statues which formed the first nucleus of the Vatican Museums collection. The **Cabinet of the Laocoon** contains the celebrated group of *Laocoon* and his sons being strangled by sea serpents which could have been inspired by one of the most famous tales from Virgil's Aeneid. This is an original work by three sculptors from the island of Rhodes, Hagesander, Athenodorus and Polydorus, and dates to 100 BC. It was found in 1506 on the Esquiline Hill. The **Cabinet of the Hermes** displays the statue of *Hermes*, a copy of an original attributed by many to Praxiteles (4th century BC). It also contains a precious Greek original dating back to the 5th century BC, representing the head of Minerva. The **Cabinet of Perseus** contains three statues sculpted by Antonio Canova to replace three ancient statues depicting the same subjects that were taken to Paris in 1800 after the signing of the Treaty of Tolentino between Pius VI and Napoleon Bonaparte. They show *Perseus* and two wrestlers, *Kreugas and Damoxenos*, sculpted according to the neo-classical ideals and faithfully inspired by the great examples of Greco-Roman art.

Next is the *Room of the Animals*, filled with statues of various kinds of animals many of which were so drastically restored in the 18th-century. On the left of the entrance is the statue of *Meleager* and his dog, a copy of the famous Greek 4th-century BC original attributed to Skopas, one of the best known artists of that time.

Proceeding to the right, the visitor reaches the long *Gallery of the Statues*. Many of them are truly remarkable. We limit ourselves to pointing out the copies of two originals by Praxiteles, the greatest Greek sculptor of the 4th century BC, the *Apollo* called *Sauroktonos* because he is shown in the act of killing a lizard and a *Silenus*, respectively in the rows on the right and on the left on entering.

This room leads into the **Gallery of the Busts**, containing an interesting series of busts many of which are Roman originals. Indeed, the Romans excelled at this type of sculp-

The helicoidal staircase in the Vatican Museums.

The oath of the Swiss Guards in St. Damaso's Courtyard.

ture. The group known as *Cato and Portia*, which dates to the first century BC and shows a Roman married couple, is famous. Returning to the Gallery of the Statues, the visitor turns right down a passage adorned with a *bas-relief* from the funerary stele of a young athlete, a precious Greek original which dates to the 5th century BC. He then enters the **Cabinet of the Masks**, a small square room elegantly decorated with mosaic paving from Hadrian's sumptuous villa near Tivoli. Indeed, the mosaics represent *theatrical masks* and a delightful *countryside scene with animals*. Alternating with precious oriental alabaster columns, four niches carved in the walls hold some of the most admired female statues of antiquity: in the center is the *Venus of Cnidos*, a beautiful copy of a famous original by Praxiteles; to the left is an elegant group representing the *Three Graces*, a copy of an original which dates to the 2nd century BC; on the left is a small copy of the graceful 3rd-century BC *crouching Venus* by the Bythnian sculptor Doidalsas.

Leaving the Gallery of the Statues and once again crossing the Room of the Animals, the visitor reaches the **Room of the Muses** which owes its name to the statues of seven of these nine famous mythological figures, patronesses of the arts, exhibited here with the statue of their leader, the god *Apollo of the Muses*. The group set against the wall consists of Roman copies of 3rd century BC Greek originals from Tivoli. In the center is the well-known **Belvedere Torso**, a highly celebrated Hellenistic fragment dating to the 1st century BC, signed by the Athenian Apollonius and discovered at the end of the 15th century in Campo de' Fiori, Rome. It is seated on a lion skin; headless and limbless, (only the thighs remain), it nonetheless demonstrates an exceptional knowledge of anatomy and a vibrant feeling of life. The greatest Renaissance artists, starting with Michelangelo and Raphael, expressed deep admiration for this fragment which is thought to portray Hercules.

The **Round Room** follows. In the center is a vast monolithic porphyry basin, more than 4 meters in diameter. Among the large-size statues standing in the wall-niches, are the famous so-called *Barberini Hera*, a copy of a Greek original of the 5th century AD, the golden age of Hellenic sculpture and the important portrait of *Antinoüs*, the Emperor Hadrian's favorite, a Roman original of the 2nd century AD. The **Greek Cross Room** follows. Here two majestic porphyry sarcophagi belonging to two eminent women of

Constantine's family are on view: the *sarcophagus of St. Helen*, the Emperor's mother, decorated with scenes of battles between Roman horsemen and barbarians and busts of Constantine and the saint, and the *sarcophagus of Constantia*, the Emperor's daughter, adorned with cupids harvesting grapes among vine tendrils.

THE VATICAN APOSTOLIC LIBRARY

The Library is divided into various sections: rooms, chapels, galleries and lastly, the Profane Museum.
The visitor first enters the **Room of Addresses of Pius IX** in the center of which the show-case displaying objects found in the excavations of Pompei in 1849 is of considerable interest.
Next to it is the circular **Chapel of St. Pius V**, whose form corresponds to that of two chapels located on the floors above and below. It contains objects from the treasury of the *Sancta Sanctorum*, the private chapel of the popes in the Lateran where important relics set in very valuable reliquaries were kept.
The **Room of the Addresses of Leo XIII** (1878-1903) and *St. Pius X* (1903-14) follows, where many letters of congratulation to these popes are kept. Continuing from the Chapel of St. Pius V, a small room can be observed on the left of the Room of the Addresses: the extremely valuable Roman fresco of the *Aldobrandini Wedding*, one of the gems of the Vatican, is preserved here.
The long gallery continues with the **Room of the Papyruses**, so called because it contains a series of papyrus scrolls of the early Middle Ages (6th-9th centuries).
The next room, the **Christian Museum**, founded by Benedict XIV in 1756, exhibits important Christian antiquities including glass, bronze, silver and ivory objects from the Roman catacombs.
This is in fact where the Library itself begins, with the Gallery of Urban VIII, which contains a collection of astronomical instruments. The two sections called the **Sistine Rooms** follow: on the dividing wall between the first and second room, on the side of the latter is a fresco portraying the *Transportation of the Obelisk to St. Peter's Square* (1586). On the right of the gallery is the great **Sistine Hall**, the heart of the library, preceded by a vestibule.

The artistic splendor of the Sistine Hall should not make the visitor forget the value of the documents exhibited in the show-cases: *manuscripts* dating to the 4th century, *palimpsests*, or in other words, ancient parchments scratched out in the Middle Ages so that new texts could be written on them, incunabula or examples of the most *ancient printed books* and *drawings and miniatures* by expert artists. Lastly, one show-case contains a large variety of *papal coins* from different periods.

The visitor then proceeds to the sections of the corridor called the **Pauline Rooms**, designed during the pontificate of Paul V, that is, in the first two decades of the 17th century. Next is the *Alexandrine Room* (called after Alexander VIII) opposite the exit of the Braccio Nuovo, which was created in 1690.

The **Clementine Gallery** follows, it owes its name to Clement XII (1730-40).

THE BORGIA APARTMENT

The six rooms forming the Borgia apartment are: 1. The room of the Sibyls; 2. The room of the Creed; 3. The room of Liberal Arts; 4. The room of the Saints; 5. The room of the Mysteries; 6. The room of the Pontiffs. Only the 4th and 5th rooms were painted by Pinturicchio. In the fourth, the most beautiful of all, the artist gracefully represented the stories of some of the martyrs: the *dispute of St. Catherine*, the *Legend of St. Barbara*, the *Legend of St. Susan*, the *Visit of St. Anthony to St. Paul the Hermit*, and the *Martyrdom of St. Sebastian*. In the fifth, the Room of the Mysteries, in the lunettes are painted the mysteries of the Resurrection, Epiphany, Nativity, Annunciation, Ascension, Pentecost and Assumption. Worthy of note in the Resurrection is the *portrait of Alexander VI*.

The apartment was built for Alexander VI Borgia (1492-1503). In 1527, during the Sack of Rome, it was seriously damaged by fierce soldiers of the Bourbons and it is to the credit of Leo XIII that he had it restored in 1889.

In 1973 Paul VI was responsible for creating a religiously-oriented **Modern Art Gallery**, using fifty-five rooms starting with the Borgia appartments. It contains more than 800 works by the most important artists from the 19th century to the present day.

The Sistine Chapel by Michelangelo. ➡

RAPHAEL ROOMS AND LOGGIAS

In 1508, while Michelangelo was beginning the decorations of the ceiling in the Sistine Chapel, Pope Julius II commissioned Raphael, who was still very young but already the idol of Patrician Rome, to cover the walls of the four vast rooms of his new residence with large frescoes.

The visit begins with the **Hall of Constantine**, reached through an external passage looking over the Belvedere Courtyard. This room is dedicated to the emperor who, in 313, decreed freedom of worship for the Christians. It was painted after the artist's death. The decoration should be attributed to his pupils Giulio Romano and Francesco Penni.

From here, a door in the wall to the left of the *Battle of Constantine* leads to **Raphael's Loggias** which face the San Damaso Courtyard. They are not open to the public; we will therefore recall only their most essential features. The general concept of the decoration is attributed to Raphael, who planned a series of biblical scenes portrayed in panels above the small vaults of the arcades (the famous Bible of Raphael). The decorative cornice inspired by the Domus Aurea (Emperor Nero's Golden House) is covered with stucco and ornamental motifs in fresco and so called "grotesques".

Access to the **Chapel of Nicholas V** is from the Hall of Constantine. It was adorned with frescoes by Beato Angelico (1448-1450) in which the master clearly narrates the stories of the two proto-martyrs Stephen and Lawrence, creating richly human scenes with great formal balance. Ornamental laurel leaves and flowers divide the frescoes on the walls into sequences on two levels.

The **Room of Heliodorus** follows. It was decorated between 1512 and 1514, by which time Raphael had completely mastered his technique. The room takes its name from the fresco on the wall of the entrance which depicts the *Expulsion of Heliodorus from the Temple in Jerusalem* for sacrilegiously attempting to steal the temple treasure. Flouting tradition, the main subject of the scene is not placed in the center, but on the left side. The central section, empty in the foreground, seems to acquire an infinite dimension with its series of arches in rhythmic succession, admist the play of light and shade. On the left, a Crowd of spectators watches the dramatic scene; behind, superbly oblivious to what is going on around them, Julius II towers, seated on his gestatorial chair with a small group of papal dignitaries.

Proceeding to the left, the visitor can admire the famous scene of the *Miracle of Bolsena*, masterfully arranged above a window. The episode illustrated took place in Bolsena in 1263: while a priest was celebrating Mass, tormented by doubts about the real presence of Christ in the consecrated host, he suddenly saw drops of blood dripping from it which stained the corporal.

On the wall opposite the entrance *Attila* (King of the Huns) *Turned Back from Rome is shown meeting St. Leo the Great*. The fourth and last scene in the Room of Heliodorus is the *Deliverance of St. Peter from Prison*. Once again the artist has found a brilliant solution to the problem created by the presence of a window: in the lunette above, the apostle's cell penetrated by an angel shining with light is portrayed. In contrast, on either side the jailers lie on two flights of steps, stunned by the impact of the heavenly messenger's sudden appearance. The background on the left is lit by a gentle moon veiled in clouds which gives the scene a touch of profound melancholy. The decoration of the room is completed by the *biblical scenes* on the ceiling attributed to Guglielmo di Marcillat, a well known 16th-century painter of stained-glass, and by the *mosaic paving*, an example of Roman art of the 2nd century AD.

The visitor then moves on into the **Room of the Segnatura**, so called because it was the meeting place of the ecclesiastical court of that name. This room was the first in which Raphael painted his frescoes, between 1509 and 1511, and it is particularly important because they are almost entirely the master's own work.

The *Disputation of the Blessed Sacrament* on the great wall opposite the entrance is a broad and serene composition, suffused with warm light.

The fresco above the window, to the left as one observes the Disputation, illustrates three of the cardinal virtues, *Fortitude*, *Prudence*, and *Temperance*; beneath, two monochromatic scenes (that is, of a single color) next to the window, represent the fourth cardinal virtue, *Justice*: on the left is the *Emperor Justinian delivering the Pandects* (civil laws) in the 6th century; on the right, *Pope Gregory IX approving the Decretals* that is, the codices of ecclesiastical law (8th century).

Sistine Chapel. The Ceiling (page 142, n. 9-8-7). ➡

On the entrance wall, opposite the Disputation, is another vast masterpiece in which Raphael's art is visibly even more fluent and mature than in the preceding fresco: the *School of Athens*, a celebration of human thought and knowledge. A vast, powerful basilica-like construction, inspired, it seems, by Bramante's project for St. Peter in the Vatican, is juxtaposed with an assembly of the greatest scholars and most learned philosophers of antiquity.

On the fourth and last wall on the right **Parnassus** is portrayed, the mythological mountain dedicated to Apollo and the nine Muses. Raphael solved the recurring problem of the presence of a window by integrating it in the view of Mount Parnassus. Apollo plays his viola in the center of the composition surrounded by the Muses and by the most famous poets of all ages, from classical antiquity to the painter's own contemporaries.

The next room is the **Room of the Fire in the Borgo**, the last to which Raphael contributed, painted between 1514 and 1517. In that period Raphael was at the peak of his activity: submerged by requests and not wishing to lose favor with the public, the master entrusted a large part of the execution of his work to his pupils, thereby lowering the technical and artistic standard of the works he had been commissioned to do.

The frescoes in this room show episodes whose protagonists are Pope Leo II and Pope Leo IV who lived in the 9th century; both are portrayed with the features of Leo X, during whose pontificate they were painted.

The most striking scene which has given the room its name is that of the *Fire in the Borgo*; it is the only one to have been entirely conceived by Raphael. Some episodes, certainly painted by the Urbinate (a native of Urbino, an epithet given to Raphael who came from that town), witness to the constantly high quality of his painting.

We will mention only some of the main frescoes in the room: on the right wall is the *Coronation of Charlemagne* by Leo III, a fresco attributed to Penni, with the assistance of Giulio Romano. On the left, is the *Naval Victory of Leo IV over the Saracens at Ostia* (849); on the window wall, the *Oath of Leo III*, by which the pontiff cleared himself of false accusations, in St. Peter's. It is attributed to Giulio Romano and by some, to Perin del Vaga.

← *Sistine Chapel. The Ceiling (page 142, n. 6-5-4).*

THE SISTINE CHAPEL

Between 1475 and 1483, Sixtus IV commissioned Giovanni de' Dolci to build the Sistine Chapel. He wanted this essential building to be architecturally isolated, virtually inaccessible from the exterior, as it were fortified.

Its decoration was begun in 1482 and it transformed the severe, almost bare chapel into a precious picture gallery of 15th- and 16th-century Italian Renaissance painting. It was Pope Sixtus IV himself who commissioned some of the best painters of the time such as Perugino, Botticelli, Ghirlandaio and Cosimo Rosselli to illustrate the parallel narratives of the Old and New Testaments which face one another on the central strip of both walls. The *Life of Moses* (Old Testament) on one side and the *Life of Christ* (New Testament) opposite, were therefore painted parallel to one another on the two lateral walls.

Thus *The Journey of Moses*, attributed to Pinturicchio, corresponds on the opposite side to the *Baptism of Jesus* which was certainly painted by Pinturicchio; in addition to the classical Christian symbolism, Roman monuments can be recognized on the hills in the background.

The next pictures are the work of Botticelli: the biblical series on the left includes *Moses with Jethro's daughters*, and in the Gospel sequence on the right, The *Temptation of Christ* and The *Healing of the Leper*.

Continuing, the *Crossing of the Red Sea* by Cosimo Rosselli, is an allegorical glorification of the great victory of the papal troops of Sixtus IV over the Neapolitans at Campomorte (1482), on the side dedicated to he Old Testament. Opposite is The *Calling of the first Apostles*, by Ghirlandaio, Michelangelo's master. Next in the sequence on one side is *Moses receiving the Tablets of the Law*, which he broke after realizing that the people of Israel were dancing round the golden calf in adoration, and on the other, *The Sermon on the Mount*, both by Rosselli.

The biblical episode of *Korah, Dathan and Abiram* is another work by Botticelli, facing *The Delivery of the Keys to St. Peter*, painted by Perugino, Raphael's master.

On the left at the end of the series of frescoes on the lateral walls we find *The Testament and Death of Moses* by Luca Signorelli, while on the right is one of Cosimo Roselli's greatest works, *The Last Supper*.

Sistine Chapel. The Ceiling (page 142, n. 3-2-1). ➡

In 1508, Julius II, ever eager for new enterprises, ordered the young Michelangelo to paint the **ceiling** of the Sistine Chapel. The gigantic work began in May 1508 and was completed on All Souls Day 1512.

The immense challenge posed by the vast size of the surface of the vault to be covered (an area of at least 800 square meters) and its bareness was brilliantly overcome by Michelangelo with an ingenuity that reveals the rich complexity of his artistic genius. In fact, he covered the actual architecture by painting over it an architectural structure in which he set the various figurative elements with an amazing three-dimensional effect.

The artist incomparably combined painting, sculpture and architecture, making the most of the curves of the vault to fit his powerful figures into the scenes.

In the center of the complex design are a sequence of nine panels showing Episodes from Genesis, from the main altar to the entrance wall. They are flanked by the famous *ignudi* (nudes) and portray respectively: the *Separation of Light and Darkness (1)*, the *Creation of the Sun and the Moon (2)*; the *Creation of Trees and Plants (3)*; the *Creation of Adam.(4)*. This is the central scene of the cycle, also from the pictorial point of view. The artist expresses the sublime act of creation by the simple touch of finger tips through which a real charge of vitality seems to flow from the Creator to Adam. The *Creation of Eve (5)* and the *Fall follow (6)*, original sin is a scene divided into two parts by the tree around which is coiled the serpent with the bust of a woman; twisting to the left, she invites Adam and Eve to pick the forbidden fruit. On the right, cause and effect are visibly related in the drama of the expulsion from the Garden of Eden. Outside the scene of earthly paradise, is *Noah's Sacrifice (7)*. This episodes celebrates his gratitude after surviving the catastrophe and is chronologically later than the following *scene of the Flood (8)*, a harmonious panel thronged with figures and episodes. Lastly, the *Drunkenness of Noah (9)* ends the powerful sequence on the vault on a note of bitter pessimism about the wretchedness of human nature.

The *Prophets and Sybils* between the triangular spaces at the curve of the vault are the largest figures in this monumental work; they are seated on solemn high-backed chairs and accompanied by angels and cherubs. *Jesus' Forefathers* are shown in the lunettes above the windows and in the tri-

← *The Last Judgment - Christ the Judge.*

angular "spandrels", while the four corner spandrels are painted with particularly dramatic *Episodes from the Old Testament*, concerning the salvation of the people of Israel. A good 23 years passed, during which the Christian world was torn apart by the Lutheran Reformation and Rome suffered the terrible Sack of 1527, before Michelangelo painted the **Last Judgement** on the wall behind the main altar. This unique masterpiece is overwhelming and dominated by the splendid audacity of its author who put his whole self into it. The Last Judgement, a compendium of the Divine Comedy and the pictorial explosion of the "Dies irae", commissioned by Pope Paul II, was begun by Michelangelo in 1535 and completed in 1541. Three hundred figures swarm in a composition which has an amazing coherence and clarity and in which space is organized into a real architectural structure of figures. Christ, the implacable judge, dominates this grandiose scene, his right arm raised in the act of condemnation. His words, "Depart from me, you cursed!" are not spoken, are not written, but they are tangibly felt. The Virgin beside him is the ever-living link between Christ and humanity. The other figures in the judgement are the prophets, apostles and the martyrs. On the Messiah's right are the elect; on his left, the damned.

Between the two lunettes, hosts of angels in heaven bring the symbols of the Passion. Below, on the left, is the scene of the resurrection of the dead: a group of angels in the center, bearing the Book of Judgement, blow trumpets, while the dead stir from gaping tombs to find themselves in the Valley of Jehoshaphat. As the good rise to heaven amidst the impotent rage of demons, the wicked are precipitated into the abysses where Charon shoves them out of his boat and Minos, the judge of hell awaits them.

Between 1980 and 1994 a large-scale restoration of the frescoes on the ceiling and the Last Judgement was carried out and attracted keen attention all over the world.

In fact, by dissolving the heavy layers of dust and lampblack deposited on the painting with the passing of centuries and the clumsy attempts at restoration with animal glues in the 17th century, somewhat unexpectedly this in-depth cleansing brought the most brilliant colors to light, which has led some experts to revise the theory of the prevalence of drawing over the use of color in Michelangelo's painting.

The Transfiguration by Raphael.

THE VATICAN PICTURE GALLERY

The pictures exposed in the Vatican Picture Gallery are of exceptional interest: they are part of a collection begun by Pope Pius VI (1775-1799) which underwent various removals before being worthily housed in this functional building. Today the Picture Gallery contains about five hundred works between pictures and tapestries, arranged in the fifteen rooms which compose it according to chronological order: from the Byzantines and early Italians of 1100-1300, whose works are exposed in the 1st room, we arrive, in fact, to the artists of 1700 and the beginning of 1800. However, the nucleus of the collection is made up by the works of the greatest masters of the Italian Renaissance, of a really inestimable value. We shall limit ourselves to noting only the principal works exposed:

1st Room - **Early Italians and Byzantines** - A notable work is the *Last Judgment* of the Roman Benedictine school of the second half of the 11th century, on a tableau of a circular shape, the work of Giovanni and Niccolò. It is one of the most ancient known pictorial representations of the Last Judgment. Of great value also is the portrait of *St. Francis* at the bottom of which we find the signature of the author, Margaritone d'Arezzo, one of the first of the painters who signed their own works. Also worthy of note are some unique little pictures of 16th century Russian art, and a *Virgin and Child* by Vitale da Bologna, a painter of the second half of the 14th century, also called "Vitale of the Madonnas". In the middle of the room we find the so-called *Cope of Boniface VIII* of the XIIIth century.

2nd Room - **Giotto and followers** - At the centre dominates the *Polyptych* (that is, a large altar painting composed in several parts) called "Stefaneschi", from the name of the Cardinal who commissioned it from Giotto, who executed it with the assistance of some of his pupils. The work, recently recomposed, at the sides represents scenes from the lives of Sts. Peter and Paul, while at the centre is the solemn figure of the benedicting Redeemer, seated on the throne between two wings of angels and adored by the same Cardinal Stefaneschi, represented below to the left. On the estrade, below the three large scenes surmounted by three gables, is represented the Madonna on the throne with the Child, flanked by two Angels and the Twelve Apostles. The back of the Polyptych, it painted too, represents St. Peter on the throne at the centre, and at the sides the Apostles St. James, St. Paul, St. Mark and St. John.

3rd Room - **Beato Angelico** - Here are exposed some very small tableaux by this famous XVth century painter, among which are two episodes of the life of *St. Nicholas of Bari*, of an almost miniature nature, and the celebrated, most delicate *Virgin and Child*, among *Sts. Domenic, Catherine and Angels*, also this one is of tiny dimensions. On the splendid gilt background sprinkled with little roses, the figure of the Virgin stands out solemn and at the same time incorporeal. The affectionate attitude of the Child, the sweet eloquence of the glances binding Mother and Son, give to the scene a sense of warm humanity. The room furthermore presents three large polyptychos, among which the two interesting ones on the side walls: on the left the *Coronation of the Virgin* by Filippo Lippi, on the right the *Virgin handing the girdle to St. Thomas* by Benozzo Gozzoli, both influenced by Angelico's art.

4th Room - **Melozzo da Forlì** - This powerful 15th century painter knew how to give deep expression to his works of the "humanistic" character of his times, which was abstracted from the vivid and working admiration for classic antiquity. The room is dominated by the large fresco which the artist had executed in the Vatican Library, later removed and placed on canvas, in order to be better kept in the Picture Gallery rooms. It represents *Sixtus IV receiving the humanist Platina*, remarkable for the psychological acuteness of the portraits of the numerous retinue, and the harmonious sense of composition. Also unforgettable are the figures of the *musician Angels and the Apostles*, coming from the frescoed decoration of the ancient apse of the church of the Holy Apostles, demolished in the 18th century to make place for a larger apse. In the room there is also exposed a vast *Flemish tapestry* of the 16th century, reproducing the *Last Supper* by Leonardo da Vinci.

5th Room - **Minor painters of the 15th century** - Besides Italian artists, the room also has Flemish, French and German painters.

6th Room - **15th century polyptychos** - There is a remarkable *Polyptych* by the Venetian Antonio Vivarini, which at
the centre shows a singular St. Anthony Abbot in "alto-rilie-
vo" of painted wood, surmounted by Christ suffering and
surrounded by various Saints. There are also some individ-
ual pictures exposed in the room, among which the lovely
Virgin and Child by the Venetian Carlo Crivelli, signed and
dated.

7th Room - **15th century Umbrian School** - The room con-
stitutes an interesting vestibule to the following room,
entirely dedicated to Raphael: it presents, in fact, works of
Umbrian artists, belonging to the same region as the great
painter, some of whom are particularly tied to him. Here in
fact are two paintings by Perugino, Raphael's master: the
Resurrection and the *Virgin and Child and four Saints*, and
a picture by Giovanni Santi, Raphael's father, representing
St. Jerome.

8th Room - **Raphael** - The room houses three of the most
famous paintings and ten tapestries of the great master from
Urbino. On the large wall in front of the entrance we can
admire the three great paintings. On the right is the
Coronation of the Virgin, an early work of the artist, painted in 1503.
On the left is the *Foligno Madonna*, which Raphael executed in Rome in 1512, at the time of the greatest splendour of
his art. The composition has become free and personal; a
rich colour animates the scene, characterised by a perfect
balance between Heaven and earth. At the centre, finally, is
exposed the celebrated **Transfiguration**, which Raphael
left unfinished at his sudden death which struck him down
in 1520, at the age of only thirty-seven. The painting was
exposed in the Sistine Chapel, before the deeply moved
Romans, during the artist's funeral. It was later completed
in the lower part, rather dark and agitated, in obvious contrast to the stupendous immateriality of the upper part, by
Giulio Romano and Francesco Penni, two of Raphael's
principal pupils.

9th Room - **Leonardo da Vinci** - The visitor is impressed
by *St. Jerome* by Leonardo da Vinci, left unfortunately
unfinished, like many, too many works of that genial artist,
writer and scientist of the Renaissance, whose uneasy and

multiform genius did not allow him to dedicate himself intensely to any activity. While on the landscape background some traces of colour are unfolded, the expressive figure of the Saint and the mighty lion nestling at his feet are only drawn on the canvas, prepared with an ochre-coloured ground. In front of this is a precious painting by another great artist who lived between the 15th and 16th centuries: the *Burial of Christ* by the Venetian Giovanni Bellini or "Giambellino", a painter considered by many as the greatest Venetian master of his times, who could mould his forms in colour, rather than model them with lines and "chiaroscuro", as had been done up to then.

10th Room - **Titian, Veronese and various 16th century artists** - The room is dominated by the immense *Madonna de' Frari*, a typical work of the most representative painter of Venice, Titian. During the long decades of his prodigious activity, the artist, who died when he was over ninety produced countless masterpieces. The Madonna de' Frari is one of these, for the wealth of its vivid and luminous colours, for the warm harmony pervading the scene, typical endowments of this great painter whom all consider a great Venetian, while in reality he was born in Pieve di Cadore. Beside this canavas is *St. Helen* by Paolo Veronese, another great exponent of the 16th century Venetian painting, the author of bright and luminous pictures.

11th Room - **Muziano and Barocci** - Among the others as Ludovico Caracci, Giorgio Vasari, Cavalier d'Arpino, Girolamo Muziano and Federico Barocci stand out, both notable representatives of the Roman artistic circle.

12th Room - **Baroque painters** - This Room, of an octagonal shape, presents paintings of considerable dimensions of the most representative figures of the 17th century. The visitor is struck above all by the *Deposition of Christ from the Cross* by Caravaggio although known through countless reproductions, the painting, seen directly, reveals a really magical luminosity which no reproduction, however perfect, could express. In that steady and sparkling light: the bodies appear carved like statues, and even the most natural and even vulgar details, for which the artist was bitterly criticised by his contemporaries, assume an aspect of incomparable nobility. Despite the lofty quality of the

Caravaggio canvas, we cannot exempt ourselves from dwelling on other very estimable works exposed in the same room: the *Crucifixion of St. Peter*, placed to the right of the Caravaggio painting, the work of Guido Reni. Another very famous painting exposed in this Room is the *Communion of St. Jerome* by Domenichino, with a theatrically scenographic composition.

13th Room - **Painters of the 17th and 18th centuries** -We note *Saint Francis Xavier* painted by the Flemish artist Anton Van Dyck, who lived for a long time in Italy before going to London, where he became the painter to the Court of Charles I, contested by all the aristocracy. Here we found the great *Virgin and Child* by Carlo Maratta and two paintings of Peter of Cortona.

14th Room - **Painters of various nationalities of the 17th and 18th centuries**. Among others, it is worth noting the painting by Pierre-Paul Rubens, one of the greatest Dutch painters of the 17th century, who lived in Italy for eight years. It represents the *Glorification of Vincenzo l Gonzaga Duke of Mantova*, at whose service the artist worked during his stay in Italy. Very popular, finally, is the *Virgin and Child* by Sassoferrato, a painter clever above all in design.

15th Room - **Portraits from the 16th to the 19th centuries** - The portraits arranged in this room represent Popes, kings and illustrious people of those centuries. We shall mention the *Portrait of the Doge Marcello*, the work of Titian, of a pure and wise line; the elegant *Portrait of George V of England* by Sir Thomas Lawrence, the great 19th century English portrait painter, principal representative of the "Regency" style; the *Portrait of Clement IX*, the masterpiece of Carlo Maratta, in which are admirable the warm symphony in red of the colour and the psychological acuteness with which the Pontiff's face is represented.

16th, 17th, 18th Rooms - **Painters of the 19th and 20th centuries**, among them we remember paintings and sculptures work of modern artists as Rodin, Fazzini, Morandi, Carrà, Greco, Manzù and Villon.

OTHER VATICAN ROOMS AND ART COLLECTIONS

The **Room of the Immaculate Conception** is richly decorated with frescoes by Podesti, interesting for its portraits of eminent persons who were present in Rome on the 8th of December 1854 when Pius IX proclaimed the dogma of the Immaculate Conception.

The **Gallery of the Candelabra** contains small statues, candelabra, valuable vases and other sculptures and mosaics. It was decorated by order of Leo XIII (1878-1903).

In the **Room of the Chariot** besides the Roman chariot of the imperial epoch, almost entirely reassembled at the end of the 18th century, there is a copy of the Discobulus in Action, found in Hadrian's Villa at Tivoli and for a long time thought to be an original by .... The head and left arm are badly restored.

The **Etruscan Museum** is a rich collection of antiquities found in various excavations in the cities of Etruria, for which the memory of the Gregory XVI will be forever honoured by all those interest in archeology.

The **Egyptian Museum** is a magnificent collection of ancient Egyptian works and objects. It was also founded by Gregory XVI.

The rest of Vatican City is a small, extraordinary universe that it is not possible to describe here, due to lack of space. We cannot however, leave out what is perhaps the most important architectural contribution of the 20th century to this exceptional comples: the great **Pontifical Audience Hall** designed by Pier Luigi Nervi (1971), which is entered through the "Arco delle Campane", for the Pope's weekly audiences and other important events.

TOURIST INFORMATION

APT, Via Parigi, 5 - ☎ 0648899253 - 06488991
ENIT, Via Marghera, 2 - ☎ 0649711
MUSEUMS AND ARCHAEOLOGICAL SITES, Information and booking
☎ 0639749907 - 0632810.
ROME MUNICIPALITY INFORMATION POINTS:
Largo Goldoni - ☎ 0668136061; Piazza San Giovanni in Laterano
☎ 0677203598; Lungotevere Castello - ☎ 0668809707; Via dei Fori
Imperiali - ☎ 0669924307; Via del Corso, 189 - ☎ 0669200435; Stazione
Termini, Piazza dei Cinquecento - ☎ 0648906300. **Hours**: 8 - 21.
THE VATICAN, Piazza San Pietro - ☎ 0669884466

HOTELS

☆☆☆☆ L

ALDROVANDI, Via U. Aldrovandi, 15 - ☎ 063223993
BERNINI BRISTOL, Piazza Barberini, 23 - ☎ 064883051
CAVALIERI HILTON, Via A. Cadlolo, 101 - ☎ 0635091
DE RUSSIE, Via Margutta, 17 - ☎ 06328881
EDEN, Via Ludovisi, 49 - ☎ 06478121
EMPIRE PALACE HOTEL, Via Aureliana, 39 - ☎ 06421281
EXCELSIOR, Via Vittorio Veneto, 125 - ☎ 0647081
HASSLER HOTEL, Piazza Trinità dei Monti, 6 - ☎ 06699340
HOLIDAY INN CROWNE, Piazza della Minerva, 69 - ☎ 06695201
LORD BYRON, Via G. De Notaris, 5 - ☎ 063220404
MAJESTIC, Via Vittorio Veneto, 50 - ☎ 06421441
PLAZA, Via del Corso, 126 - ☎ 0669921111
REGINA HOTEL BAGLIONI, Via Vittorio Veneto, 72 - ☎ 06427777
ST. REGIS (Grand Hotel), Via Vittorio Emanuele Orlando, 3 - ☎ 064709

☆☆☆☆

AMBASCIATORI PALACE, Via Vittorio Veneto, 62 - ☎ 0647493
ANGLO-AMERICANO, Via Quattro Fontane, 12 - ☎ 06472941
ATLANTE GARDEN, Via Crescenzio, 78/a - ☎ 066872361
ATLANTE STAR, Via G. Vitelleschi, 34 - ☎ 066873233
BAROCCO, Via della Purificazione, 4 - ☎ 064872001
BERNINI-BRISTOL, Piazza Barberini, 23 - ☎ 064883051
BEVERLY-HILLS, Largo B. Marcello, 220 - ☎ 068542141
BORROMINI, Via Lisbona, 7 - ☎ 068841321
CARDINAL, Via Giulia, 62 - ☎ 0668802719
CICERONE, Via Cicerone, 55/c - ☎ 063576
CLARIDGE, Viale Liegi, 62 - ☎ 068419212
DE LA VILLE, Via Sistina, 67 - ☎ 0667331
DEI BORGOGNONI, Via Del Bufalo, 126 - ☎ 0669941505
(THE) DUKE HOTEL, Via Archimede, 69 - ☎ 06367221
ELISEO, Via di Porta Pinciana, 30 - ☎ 064870456
ERGIFE PALACE, Via Aurelia, 619 - ☎ 0666440

FARNESE, Via Alessandro Farnese, 30 - ☎ 063212553
FLORA, Via Vittorio Veneto, 191 - ☎ 06489929
FORUM, Via Tor de' Conti, 25 - ☎ 066792446
GIULIO CESARE, Via degli Scipioni, 287 - ☎ 063210751
HILTON ROME AIRPORT, Via Fratelli Wright - ☎ 065251
HOLIDAY-INN - St. PETER'S, Via Aurelia Antica, 415 - ☎ 0666420
IMPERATOR, Via Aurelia, 619 - ☎ 06664180410
IMPERIALE, Via Vittorio Veneto, 24 - ☎ 064826351
JOLLY-HOTEL, Corso Italia, 1 - ☎ 068495
LEONARDO DA VINCI, Via dei Gracchi, 324 - ☎ 0632499
LONDRA & CARGILL, Piazza Sallustio, 18 - ☎ 06473871
MASSIMO D'AZEGLIO, Via Cavour, 18 - ☎ 064620561
MEDITERRANEO, Via Cavour, 15 - ☎ 064884051
MEMPHIS, Via degli Avignonesi, 36 - ☎ 06485849
MIDAS-PALACE, Via Aurelia, 800 - ☎ 0666396
MONDIAL, Via Torino, 127 - ☎ 06472861
NAZIONALE, Piazza Montecitorio, 131 - ☎ 06695001
NOVA DOMUS, Via G. Savonarola, 33 - ☎ 0639732955
PALATINO, Via Cavour, 213 - ☎ 064814927
PARCO MEDICI, Via Castello della Magliana, 65 - ☎ 0665581
PARK HOTEL COSTANZA, Via Cristoforo Colombo, 1500 - ☎ 06520971
PINETA PALACE, Via S. Lino Papa, 35 - ☎ 063013800
PISANA PALACE, Via della Pisana, 374 - ☎ 0666690
PLAZA, Via del Corso, 126 - ☎ 0669921111
PRESIDENT, Via Emanuele Filiberto, 173 - ☎ 06770121
PRINCESS, Via A. Ferrara, 33 - ☎ 06664931
QUIRINALE, Via Nazionale, 7 - ☎ 064707
REGINA HOTEL BAGLIONI, Via Vittorio Veneto, 72 - ☎ 06476851
RITZ, Via Chelini, 41 - ☎ 068083751
RIVOLI, Via T. Taramelli, 7 - ☎ 063224042
ROYAL SANTINA, Via Marsala, 22 - ☎ 064455241
SAVOY HOTEL, Via Ludovisi, 15 - ☎ 064744141
SHERATON, Viale del Pattinaggio - ☎ 065453
SHERATON GOLF, Viale Parco dei Medici, 167 - ☎ 0665858741
SUMMIT, Via della Stazione Aurelia, 99 - ☎ 0666418028
VILLA PAMPHILI, Via della Nocetta, 105 - ☎ 066602
VISCONTI PALACE, Via Cesi, 37 - ☎ 063684

☆☆☆

ACCADEMIA, Piazza Accademia di San Luca, 75 - ☎ 0669922603
AMALFI, Via Merulana, 278 - ☎ 064744313
ARA PACIS, Via Vittoria Colonna, 11 - ☎ 063204446
ARCANGELO, Via Boezio, 15 - ☎ 066874143
ARCHIMEDE, Via dei Mille, 19 - ☎ 064452378
ARISTON, Via F. Turati, 16 - ☎ 064465399
ASTRID, Largo Antonio Sarti, 4 - ☎ 063236371
AUGUSTEA, Via Nazionale, 251 - ☎ 064883589
BARRETT, Largo Torre Argentina, 47 - ☎ 066868481
BUENOS AIRES, Via Clitunno, 9 - ☎ 068554854

CANOVA, Via Urbana, 10a - ☎ 064873314
CARRIAGE, Via delle Carrozze, 36 - ☎ 066990124
CELIO, Via SS. Quattro, 35 - ☎ 0670495333
CITY HOTEL, Via Due Macelli, 97 - ☎ 066797468
CLODIO, Via Santa Lucia, 10 - ☎ 063721122
COLUMBUS, Via della Conciliazione, 33 - ☎ 066865435
CONSUL, Via Aurelia, 727 - ☎ 0666418051
COROT, Via Marghera, 17 - ☎ 0644700900
DELLA CONCILIAZIONE, Borgo Pio, 164 - ☎ 066867910
DIANA, Via Principe Amedeo, 4 - ☎ 064827541
DOVER, Via della Pineta Sacchetti, 43 - ☎ 066622818
FIAMMA, Via Gaeta, 61 - ☎ 064818436
FONTANA, Piazza di Trevi, 96 - ☎ 066786113
GENIO, Via Zanardelli, 28 - ☎ 0668307246
GERBER, Via degli Scipioni, 241 - ☎ 063221001
IMPERATOR, Via Aurelia, 619 - ☎ 0666418041
INTERNAZIONALE, Via Sistina, 79 - ☎ 066793047
KING, Via Sistina, 131 - ☎ 064880878
LA RESIDENZA, Via Emilia, 22 - ☎ 064880789
MARCELLA, Via Flavia, 104 - ☎ 0642014591
MIAMI, Via Nazionale, 230 - ☎ 064817180
MILANI, Via Magenta, 12 - ☎ 064457051
OXFORD, Via Boncompagni, 89 - ☎ 064203601
PICCADILLY, Via Magna Grecia, 122 - ☎ 0670474858
PINCIO, Via Capo le Case, 50 - ☎ 066790758
PORTAMAGGIORE, Piazza Porta Maggiore, 25 - ☎ 067027927
RIVER, Via Flaminia, 39 - ☎ 063200841
SANT'ANNA, Borgo Pio, 133 - ☎ 0668801602
SANT'ANSELMO, Piazza S. Anselmo, 2 - ☎ 065743547
SANTA MAURA, Via Casilina, 1038 - ☎ 062674041
TEATRO DI POMPEI, Largo del Pallaro, 8 - ☎ 0668300170
TREVI, Vicolo del Babuccio, - ☎ 066789563
TRINITA' DEI MONTI, Via Sistina, 91 - ☎ 066797206
VIMINALE, Via C. Balbo, 31 - ☎ 064881910
YORK, Via Cavriglia, 26 - ☎ 068102222

CAMPINGS

AURELIA CLUB - Via Castel di Guido, 541 - ☎ 066689039
CAPITOL - Via Castel Fusano, 45 (Ostia Antica) - ☎ 065650621
COUNTRY CLUB Castel Fusano - P. Castel Fusano, 1 - ☎ 065662710
FABULOUS - Via C. Colombo, km 18 - ☎ 065259354
FLAMINIO - Via Flaminia Nuova, km 831 - ☎ 063332604
HAPPY - Via Prato della Corte, 1915 - ☎ 0633626401
ROMA - Via Aurelia, km 8,100 - ☎ 066623018
ROMAN RIVER - Via Tenuta Piccirilli, 207 - ☎ 0633613263
SEVEN HILLS - Via Cassia, 1216 - ☎ 0630310826
TIBER - Via Tiberina, km 1,400 - ☎ 0633612314

RESTAURANTS AND "TRATTORIE"

In the restaurants marked with ★ one spends no more than 21/26 euro.
In the restaurants marked with ★★ one spends from 26 to 35 euro.
In the restaurants marked with ★★★ one spends from 36 to 50 euro.
In the restaurants marked with ★★★★ one spends more than 52 euro.

★★★★ **Agata e Romeo**, Via Carlo Alberto, 45 - ☎ 064466115
★★★★ **Alberto Ciarla**, Piazza San Cosimato, 40 - ☎ 065818668
★★★★ **Andrea**, Via Sardegna, 26 - ☎ 064821891
★★★★ **Antico Arco,** Piazzale Aurelio, 7 - ☎ 065815274
★★ 　　 **Bacaro**, Via degli Spagnoli, 27 - ☎ 066864110
★★★ 　 **(Dal) Bolognese**, Piazza del Popolo, 1 - ☎ 063611426
★★★★ **Camponeschi**, Piazza Farnese, 50 - ☎ 066874927
★★ 　　 **(Il) Cardinale**,Via delle Carceri, 6 - ☎ 066869336
★★ 　　 **Celestina ai Parioli**, Viale Parioli, 184 - ☎ 068078242
★★★ 　 **(Al) Ceppo**, Via Panama, 2 - ☎ 068419696
★★ 　　 **Cesarina**, Via Piemonte, 109 - ☎ 064880828
★★★ 　 **Charly's Sauciere**, Via S. Giovanni in Laterano, 270 - ☎ 0670494700
★★★★ **Checchino dal 1887**, Via Monte Testaccio, 30 - ☎ 065746318
★★ 　　 **Checco er Carrettiere**, Via Benedetta, 10 - ☎ 065817018
★★ 　　 **(Al) Chianti**, Via Ancona, 17 - ☎ 0644250242
★ 　　　 **(Il) Colonnato**, Piazza Sant'Uffizio, 678 - ☎ 066865371
★★ 　　 **Colline Emiliane**,Via degli Avignonesi, 22 - ☎ 064817538
★★★ 　 **Consolini**, Via Marmorata, 28 - ☎ 0657300148
★★★ 　 **(Il) Convivio**, Via dell'Orso, 44 - ☎ 066869432
★★★★ **Coriolano**, Via Ancona, 14 - ☎ 0644249863
★★ 　　 **(Il) Cortiletto**, Piazza Capranica, 77 -☎ 066793977
★★★ 　 **Costanza**, Piazza del Paradiso, 65 - ☎ 066861717
★★★ 　 **(La) Dolce Vita**, L.Tevere di Pietra Papa, 51 - ☎ 065579865
★★ 　　 **(Il) Drappo**, Vicolo del Malpasso, 9 - ☎ 066877365
★ 　　　 **(L') Eau Vive**, Via Monterone, 85 - ☎ 0668801095
★★ 　　 **Edoardo**, Via Locullo, 2 - ☎ 06486428
★★★ 　 **(L') Elite**, Via Salaria, 1223, ☎ 068804503
★★★★ **(Les) Etoiles**, Via Vitelleschi, 34 - ☎ 066873233
★★★ 　 **Evangelista**, Via delle Zoccolette, 11a - ☎ 066875810
★★★ 　 **Fabrizio a Santa Dorotea**, Via S. Dorotea, 15 - ☎ 065806244
★★ 　　 **Fantasie di Trastevere**, Via Santa Dorotea, 6 - ☎ 065894984
★★★ 　 **Fortunato**, Via del Pantheon, 55 - ☎ 066792788
★★ 　　 **(La) Gallina Bianca**, Via Antonio Rosmini, 9 - ☎ 064743777
★★★ 　 **Giovanni**, Via Marche, 64 - ☎ 064821834
★★ 　　 **Girarrosto dal Toscano**, Via Germanico, 58 - ☎ 0639725717
★★ 　　 **(Da) Giuseppe**, Via A. Brunetti, 59 - ☎ 063219019
★★★ 　 **'Gusto**, Piazza Augusto Imperatore, 9 - ☎ 063226273
★★ 　　 **(La) Lampada**, Via Quintino Sella, 25 - ☎ 064744323
★ 　　　 **(Da) Lucia**, Vicolo del Mattonato, 2b - ☎ 065803601
★ 　　　 **(Da) Margherita**, Piazza delle Cinque Scole, 30 - ☎ 066864002

★★★ **Mariano**, Via Piemonte, 79 - ☎ 064745256

★★ **(Le) Maschere**, Via Monte della Farina, 29 - ☎ 066879444

★★ **Massimo D'Azeglio**, Via Cavour, 14 - ☎ 064814101

★★ **(Il) Matriciano**, Via dei Gracchi, 55 - ☎ 063212327

★ **Maurizio**, Via Marghera, 39 - ☎ 06491230

★★★ **Méditerranée**, Via Fauro, 2 - ☎ 0680663694

★★ **Nino**, Via Borgognona, 11 - ☎ 066795676

★★★ **Osteria dell'Antiquario**, P.zza San Simeone, 27 - ☎ 066879694

★★ **Osteria dell'ingegno**, Piazza di Pietra, 45 - ☎ 066780662

★★ **Osteria Picchioni**, Via del Boschetto, 16 - ☎ 064885261

★★★★ **Papà Baccus**, Via Toscana, 36 - ☎ 0642742808

★★★ **Papà Giovanni**, Via dei Sediari, 6 - ☎ 0668804807

★★★ **Passetto**, Via Zanardelli, 14 - ☎ 0668803696

★★ **Peccati di Gola**, Piazza de' Ponziani, 7A - ☎ 065814529

★ **Perilli a Testaccio**, Via Marmorata, 39 - ☎ 065742415

★★★★ **(La) Pergola - Cavalieri Hilton**, V. Cadlolo, 101 - ☎ 0635092152

★★ **(Il) Piacere**, Via G. Animuccia, 16 - ☎ 068606259

★★★ **Piperno**, Via Monte dè Cenci, 9 - ☎ 0668806629

★★ **Pizzaré**, Via Lucullo, 22 - ☎ 0642013075

★★ **Pommidoro**, Piazza dei Sanniti, 44 - ☎ 064452692

★ **(Al) Pompiere**, Via S. Maria dei Calderari, 38 - ☎ 0668803142

★★ **Porto di Ripetta**, Via di Ripetta, 250 - ☎ 063612376

★★ **(Il) Posto Accanto**, Via del Boschetto, 36A - ☎ 064743002

★★ **Pulcinella**, Via Urbana, 11 - ☎ 064743310

★★ **(Il) Quadrifoglio**, Via del Boschetto, 19 - ☎ 064826096

★★ **Quattro Fiumi**, Piazza Navona, 37 - ☎ 066864028

★★★★ **Relais la Piscine**, Via G. Mangili, 6 - ☎ 063223993

★★★★ **Relais le Jardin**, Via G. De Notaris, 5 - ☎ 063224541

★★★ **Robià**, Via Cicerone, 55 - ☎ 063576

★★ **Romolo**, Via di Porta Settimiana, 8 - ☎ 065818284

★★★★ **(La) Rosetta**, Via della Rosetta, 8/9 - ☎ 066861002

★★★ **San Luigi**, Via Mocenigo, 10 - ☎ 0639720704

★★★★ **Sans Souci**, Via Sicilia, 20 - ☎ 064821814

★ **Scoglio di Frisio**, Via Merulana, 256 - ☎ 064872765

★★★ **Severino a Piazza Zama**, Piazza Zama, 5 - ☎ 0670003901

★★ **(La) Tana del Grillo**, Via Alfieri, 4 - ☎ 0670453517

★★★ **Taverna Angelica**, Piazza delle Vaschette, 14A - ☎ 066874514

★★ **Taverna Flavia**, Via Flavia, 9 - ☎ 064870483

★ **Taverna Giulia**, Vicolo dell'Oro, 23 - ☎ 066869768

★★ **Terra di Siena**, Piazza Pasquino, 77 - ☎ 0668307704

★★★★ **(La) Terrazza dell'Eden**, Via Ludovisi, 49 - ☎ 06478121

★★ **(Dal) Toscano**, Via Germanico, 56 - ☎ 0639725717

★★★★ **(El) Toulà**, Via della Lupa, 29b - ☎ 066873498

★ **Trattoria Monti**, Via S. Vito, 13 - ☎ 064466573

★★ **(Al) 34**, Via Mario dè Fiori, 34 - ☎ 066795091

★★ **(Il) Valentino**, Via della Fontanella, 15 - ☎ 063610880

★★★ **Vecchia Roma**, Via Tribuna di Campitelli, 18 - ☎ 066864604

TRANSPORT

SIGHTSEEING TOUR OF THE CITY - Line 110

Leaves from Termini Station, Piazza dei Cinquecento, every 30 minutes, 10:00 a.m. - 6:00 p.m., October1 - March 31; 9:00 a.m. - 8:00 p.m. April 1 - September 30. Ticket € 7,75.

BUS UNDERGROUND AND URBAN RAILWAYS

ATAC - TRAMBUS - METRO - COTRAL
From 8:00 a.m. to 6:00 p.m., except Saturday ☎ 800431784

NATIONAL STATE RAILWAYS

User's Information Office- ☎ 848888088
web-site: www.fs-online.it
Lost & found- ☎ 0647306682
Handicapped assistance - ☎ 064881726

AIRPORTS

"Leonardo Da Vinci" Intercontinental Airport of Fiumicino - ☎ 0665951 - 0665953640-65955237
Ciampino Airport - ☎ 067949.41

CONNECTION WITH AIRPORTS

TRAINS TO/FROM FIUMICINO AIRPORT *(FS)*
Roma Tiburtina Station - Tuscolana Station - Ostiense Station - Trastevere Station - Magliana Station - Muratella - **Airport Leonardo Da Vinci - Fiumicino.**
Ticket € 4,65. Departures every 15 minutes, from 5,06 a.m. to 10,36 p.m.

DIRECT LINE, Rome Termini Station (Platforms 25/27) **- L. Da Vinci Airport in Fiumicino**
Ticket € 8,78. Departures from **Termini Station**, from 6,50 a.m. and from 7,20 a.m. to 9,20 p.m. Trips last approx. 60 minutes.
Departures from Fiumicino, from 7,37 a.m. and from 8,07 a.m. to 10,07 p.m. Trips last approx. 60 minutes.

BUSES TO/FROM CIAMPINO AIRPORT: Every 30 minutes from/to **Anagnina Metro Station** of line A, from 5,30 a.m. to 11,00 p.m.

TAXIS

RADIOTAXIS:
☎ 068822 - 066645 - 064157 - 063570 - 064994 - 064994

Rates: To go to **"Leonardo Da Vinci" Intercontinental Airport of Fiumicino** the base city rate is added a € 7,23 supplement.
From the Airport to Rome, a € 5,94 supplement is added to the rate indicated above.

Rates for Ciampino International Airport: to the base city rate is added a € 5,16 supplement.

TAXI RATES VALID FOR THE METROPOLITAN AREA:
Initial fixed rate at time of departure:
7:00 a.m. - 10:00 p.m., € 2,33
10:00 p.m. - 7:00 a.m., € 3,36
Weekends/holidays 7:00 a.m. - 10:00 p.m., € 4,91

Supplements: bagage € 1,03 (min. size: cm 35X25X80) - night-time service (from 10:00 p.m. to 7:00 a.m.) € 2,58 - Day-time service on holidays: € 1,03.

MONUMENTS

BATHS OF CARACALLA, Via delle di Terme di Caracalla. ☎ 065758626. Ticket € 5,00. Hours: from 9 a.m. to 3,30 p.m. On Mondays from 9 a.m. to 1 p.m.

COLOSSEUM, Piazza del Colosseo. ☎ 067005469. Ticket € 8,00. Hour: Winter 9 a.m.-3,30 p.m.; Summer 9 a.m.-6 p.m.

DOMUS AUREA, Viale della Domus Aurea - Colle Oppio. Visits by reservation only ☎ 0639967700. Entrance € 6,00. Hours: 9 a.m.- 7,45 p.m.

MONUMENT TO VITTORIO EMANUELE II, Piazza Venezia.

PALATIN, Largo Romolo e Remo, 5 and Via San Gregorio, 30. ☎ 066990110. Ticket € 6,20. Hours: from 9 a.m. to one hour before the sunset.

PANTHEON, Piazza della Rotonda. ☎ 0668300230. Free entrance. Hours: 8,30 a.m.-7,30 p.m.; Sunday 9 a.m.-6 p.m.

ROMAN FORUM, Largo Romolo e Remo, 5. ☎ 066990110. Free entrance. Hours: from 9 a.m. to one hour before the sunset.

RUINS OF OSTIA ANTICA. Via dei Romagnoli, 717 - Ostia Antica. ☎ 0656358099. Ticket: € 4,13. Hours: Winter 8,30 a.m.-5p.m.; Summer 9a.m.-6p.m. Closed on Mondays.

TRAJAN'S MARKETS, Via IV Novembre, 94. ☎ 066790048. Ticket € 6,20. Hours: 9 a.m.-4,30 p.m.; Summer: 9 a.m.-6,30 p.m. Closed on Mondays.

MUSEUMS AND GALLERIES

ANCIENT ART NATIONAL GALLERY (Palazzo Barberini), Via Barberini, 18. ☎ 0632810 - 064814591. Ticket € 6,19. Hours: 9 a.m.-7,30 p.m. Saturday 9 a.m.-11p.m. Closed on Mondays.

AULA OTTAGONA (Roman National Museum), Via G. Romita, 8. ☎ 064870690. Free entrance. Hours: 9a.m.-2p.m. Sundays 9a.m.-1p.m. Closed on Mondays.

BARRACCO ANCIENT SCULPTURE MUSEUM, Via dei Baullari, 1. ☎ 0668806848. Ticket € 5,16. Hours: 9 a.m.-7 p.m.; Sunday 9 a.m.-1 p.m. Closed on Mondays.

BIOPARCO (Zoo), Viale del Giardino Zoologico,20/22. ☎ 063608211. Ticket € 7,50. Cut price tickets € 5,50. Hours: 8,30 a.m.-1 p.m. and 2,40 p.m.-5 p.m.

BORGHESE GALLERY AND MUSEUM. Piazzale Scipione Borghese, 5. Tel. 068548577. Visits by reservation only ☎ 0632810. Ticket € 6,19. Hours: 9 a.m.-7,30 p.m. Saturday 9a.m.-11p.m. Closed on Mondays.

CAPITOLINI MUSEUMS, Piazza del Campidoglio. ☎ 0639967800. Ticket € 7,74. Hours: 9 a.m. -8 p.m. Closed on Mondays.

CASTEL SANT'ANGELO, Lgt. Castello, 1. ☎ 0639967600. Ticket € 5,16. Hours: 9 a.m.-8 p.m. Saturday 9 a.m. - 11 p.m. Closed on Mondays.

DORIA PAMPHILI GALLERY, Piazza del Collegio Romano, 2. ☎ 066797323. Ticket € 7,30. Hours: 10 a.m.-5 p.m. Closed on Thursday.

ETRUSCAN NATIONAL MUSEUM, Piazzale di Villa Giulia, 9. ☎ 063226571. Ticket € 4,13. Hours: 8,30 a.m.-7,30 p.m., Sundays 9 a.m.-2 p.m.; Closed on Mondays.

EXPLORA, The Children's Museum. Via Flaminia, 80. ☎ 063613776. Ticket € 5,16. Tours last 1 hour and 45 minutes, starting at 9,30 -11,30 a.m. - 3 and 5 p.m. Saturdays and holidays 10 a.m., 12 Noon, 3 and 5p.m.

MODERN ART NATIONAL GALLERY, Viale Belle Arti, 131. ☎ 06322981. Ticket € 6,19. Hours: 8,30 a.m.-7,30 p.m.; Saturday 9 a.m.-11 p.m. Closed on Mondays.

PALAZZO ALTEMPS (Roman National Museum), Piazza Sant'Apollinare. ☎ 066833759. Ticket € 5,16. Hours: 9 a.m.-6,45 p.m. Sunday 9 a.m.-7,45 p.m. Closed on Mondays.

PALAZZO DELLE ESPOSIZIONI, Via Nazionale, 194. ☎ 064745903. Ticket € 7,75. Hours: 10 a.m.-9 p.m. Closed on Tuesday.

PALAZZO MASSIMO (Roman National Museum), Largo Villa Peretti,1. ☎ 0639080730. Ticket € 6,19. Hours: 9a.m.-6,45p.m. Sunday 9a.m.-7,45p.m. Closed on Mondays.

PALAZZO VENEZIA, Via del Plebiscito, 118. ☎ 066798865. Ticket € 4,13. Hours 9 a.m.-2 p.m. On Sundays from 9 a.m. to 1 p.m.

PREHISTORIC AND ETHNOLOGICAL MUSEUM, Piazza G. Marconi, 14. ☎ 06549521. Ticket € 4,13. Hours: 9 a.m.-8 p.m.; Closed on Mondays.

ROMAN CIVILIZATION MUSEUM, Piazza G. Agnelli, 10 (Eur). ☎ 065926041.Ticket € 4,13. Hours: 9 a.m.-6,30 p.m.; Sunday 9 a.m.-1,30 p.m. Closed on Mondays.

SPADA GALLERY, Piazza Capo di Ferro, 3. ☎ 0632810 - 066861158. Ticket € 5,16. Free entrance under 18 and over 60 years old. Hours: 8,30 a.m.-7,30 p.m. Closed on Mondays.

VATICAN MUSEUMS , Viale Vaticano. ☎ 066988.3333. Ticket € 9,26. Hours: 8,45 a.m.-12,20 p.m. Closed on Sundays. Free entrance last sunday of every month. Visits to Vatican Gardens call Tel. 0669884466.

BASILICAS

ST. JOHN LATERAN, Piazza San Giovanni. ☎ 0669886464.
ST. MARY MAJOR, Piazza Santa Maria Maggiore. ☎ 064881094.
ST. PAUL OUTSIDE THE WALLS, Piazzale San Paolo. ☎ 065410341.
ST. PETER IN THE VATICAN, Piazza San Pietro . ☎ 0669883462.

MAIN CHURCHES

HOLY CROSS IN JERUSALEM, Piazza S. Croce in Gerusalemme, 12. Hours: 7 a.m.-7,15 p.m. ☎ 067014769

ST. AGNES IN AGONE, Piazza Navona. Hours: 5 p.m.-6,30 p.m. On Sundays 10 a.m.-1 p.m. ☎ 066794435.

SAN CLEMENT, Piazza San Clemente. Hours: 9 a.m.-12 a.m., 3,30 p.m.-6 p.m. ☎ 0670451018.

ST. LAWRENCE OUTSIDE THE WALLS, Piazzale del Verano, 3. Hours: 7,30 a.m.-12 a.m., 3 p.m.-7 p.m. ☎ 06491511

ST. MARY DEL POPOLO, Piazza del Popolo. Hours: 7 a.m.-12 a.m., 4 p.m.-7 p.m. ☎ 063610836.

ST. MARY OF THE ANGELS, Piazza della Repubblica. ☎ 064880812. Hours: 10,30 a.m.-12 a.m., 4 p.m.-7 p.m.

ST. MARY IN ARACOELI, Piazza Aracoeli. ☎ 066798155. Hours: 7-12 a.m., 4 p.m.-5,30 p.m.

ST. MARY IN COSMEDIN, Piazza Bocca della Verità. ☎ 066781419. Hours; 9a.m.-1p.m., 3p.m.-6p.m.

ST. MARY IN TRASTEVERE, Piazza Santa Maria in Trastevere ☎ 065814802. Hours: 7a.m.-1 p.m., 4 p.m.-7 p.m.

ST. PETER IN VINCOLI, Piazza S. Pietro in Vincoli. ☎. 064882865. Hours: 7 a.m.-12,30 a.m., 3,30 p.m.-6 p.m.

SCALA SANTA, Piazza S. Giovanni in Laterano. ☎ 0670494489. Hours: 6,15 a.m.-12 a.m.; 3,30 p.m.-6,30 p.m.

TRINITÀ DEI MONTI, Piazza Trinità dei Monti.

CATACOMBS

DOMITILLA, Via delle Sette Chiese, 280. ☎ 065110342.
PRISCILLA, Via Salaria, 430. ☎ 0686206272.
ST. AGNES, Via Nomentana, 349. ☎ 068610840
ST. CALIXTUS, Via Appia Antica, 110. ☎ 065136725.
ST. SEBASTIAN, Via Appia Antica, 136. ☎ 067887035.

SHOPPING

TIME SCHEDULE:

Winter season (from October to March): from 9,00 a.m. to 1,00 p.m. and from 3,30 p.m. to 7,30 p.m. Some shops in the centre of the City are open no-stop from 10,30 a.m. to 7,30 p.m. Shops are close on Mondays mornings. The grocery stores are closed on Thursdays afternoons and specialised stores are closed on Saturday afternoons.

Summer season (from April to September): from 9,00 a.m. to 1,00 p.m. and from 4,00 p.m. to 8,00 p.m. During the Summer season the shops are closed on Saturdays afternoons. In every month of the year shops are mostly closed on Sunday days.

Via Condotti: clothes, shoes and jewellry from the most famous Italian and foreign designers, such as Armani (n. 76), Prada (n. 92), Gucci (n. 8), Bulgari (n. 10), Cartier (n. 82/83), Ferragamo (n. 65 and 73), Max Mara (n. 19), Campanile (n. 58), Beltrami (n. 78) Valentino for woman (n. 13). And in **Via Bocca di Leone**, a side street, you'll find Valentino (n. 15) and Gianni Versace (n. 26).

Piazza di Spagna: if we manage to tear our gaze away from the magnificent spectacle of the splendid square and its incomparable stairway we can recognize the shop windows of some of the best known boutiques selling clothing, leather goods and shoes, among which we find Genny (n. 27), Missoni (n. 78), Les Copains (n. 35) e Dolce e Gabbana (n. 82).

Via Borgognona: clothes and shoes of the greatest Italian fashion designers, such as Fendi (n. 39), Ferré (n. 6), Laura Biagiotti (n. 43), Polidori (n. 4/A), Versace for man (n. 24), Moschino (n. 82), Fratelli Rossetti, shoes, (n. 5a).

Via Frattina: clothes, shoes, purses, perfumes, such as Byblos (n. 34a), Castelli (n. 52), Max Mara (n. 28), Pollini (n. 22).

Via del Corso: clothes, shoes, jeans.

Via del Babuino: antiques and clothing, such as Oliver (n.61), Armani (n.140) and Tiffany (n. 118).

Via Cola di Rienzo: clothes, shoes.

Porta Portese:characteristic flea market full of all kinds of antique, used and new items. Opens every Sunday morning in the streets around Porta Portese.

TAX FREE SHOPPING

Tourists arriving from countries not belonging to the European Union can request the refund of I.V.A. (V.A.T. which ranges from 12% to 35% on purchase price) for amounts exceeding 155,00 euro spent in the same shop.
To enjoy this benefit it's necessary to apply to shops that have an agreement with the organisations offering the service (Tax Free, Italy Free Shopping, Tax Free System, Euro Tax, Tax Refund). The refund can be obtained inside the shops with the proper sign, at Leonardo Da Vinci International Airport of Fiumicino, in the Customs office, or by post.

EMERGENCY TELEPHONE NUMBERS

☎

```
POLICE - EMERGENCY ..............................................................................113
CARABINIERI ..........................................................................................112
TRAFFIC & HIGHWAY POLICE .............................................................065544
ITALIAN RED CROSS (CRI) AMBULANCE .......................................065510
FIRE BRIGADE..........................................................................................115
MUNICIPAL POLICE ..........................................................................0667691
POLICE HEADQUARTERS ................................................................064686
FIRST-AID..................................................................................................118
CITIZENS' EMERGENCY.....................................................................0647498
```